TRANSLATIONS FROM GREEK AND ROMAN AUTHORS

Series Editor : GRAHAM TINGAY

Empire and Emperors

Selections from Tacitus' Annals

Translated by

GRAHAM TINGAY

Head of Classics, King's College School, Wimbledon

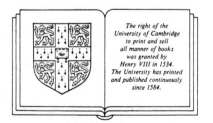

The right of the
University of Cambridge
to print and sell
all manner of books
was granted by
Henry VIII in 1534.
The University has printed
and published continuously
since 1584.

CAMBRIDGE UNIVERSITY PRESS

Cambridge
London   New York   New Rochelle
Melbourne   Sydney

CAMBRIDGE UNIVERSITY PRESS
Cambridge, New York, Melbourne, Madrid, Cape Town, Singapore, São Paulo, Delhi

Cambridge University Press
The Edinburgh Building, Cambridge CB2 8RU, UK

Published in the United States of America by Cambridge University Press, New York

www.cambridge.org
Information on this title: www.cambridge.org/9780521281904

© Cambridge University Press 1983

First published 1983
Reprinted 1986
Re-issued in this digitally printed version 2008

A catalogue record for this publication is available from the British Library

Library of Congress Catalogue Card Number: 82–14616

ISBN 978-0-521-28190-4 paperback

Maps by Reg Piggott

Cover design by Ken Farnhill. The photographs on the cover show five of the Roman
emperors whose reigns are described by Tacitus: top left, Nero; top right, Claudius;
centre, Augustus; bottom left, Caligula; bottom right, Tiberius. Reproduced by courtesy
of the Mansell Collection.

Contents

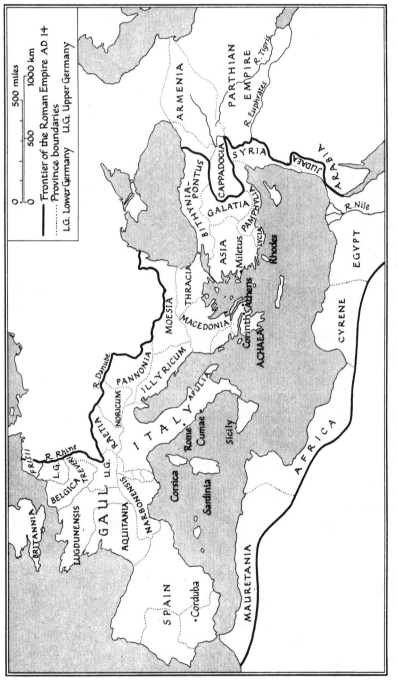

The Roman empire in the reign of Tiberius

Introduction: Tacitus and history

ROME – FROM REPUBLIC TO EMPIRE

On the Ides of March, 15 March, 44 BC, Julius Caesar was stabbed to death in the centre of Rome. While thirty-five blows fell on his body, not a soul moved to help him: his body lay untouched till his slaves came to fetch it home. Sixty of Rome's most influential citizens, led by Brutus and Cassius, had planned the killing. They were not criminals; many of them were Caesar's friends, most of them were honourable men. To discover why they killed Caesar, we must look back briefly some two hundred years.

By military conquest or shrewd alliance, Rome had united nearly all of Italy and brought it firmly under her control; in 241 BC, after a long and gruelling war, she won her first possession overseas, the island of Sicily. Corsica and Sardinia were the next provinces, as these foreign possessions were called, added within a couple of years. By 130 BC, Rome had acquired a large empire and governed many of the countries around the Mediterranean. Industry and trade flourished, and wealth poured into Rome. Despite these changes Rome was still a city with a city's republican government, in which there was a sort of balance between the senate, the magistrates and the people. There were no representatives from the provinces or other towns of Italy to share in the government.

The senate[1] was the main governing council of the state. Its three hundred members were chosen, by two of its senior members, from the sons of senators, and from junior magistrates[2] elected by the people; once selected, senators served for life. The senior magistrates were the executive officials of the republic; they were the two consuls[3] and the praetors,[4] whose numbers increased over the years from two to eight. They were all elected annually by the people, though there was in fact little choice, for only members of the senate could become consuls or praetors. They carried out the civil business of the state, and also commanded its armies when there was a war, and governed its provinces in peace. Laws were passed in the senate, supposedly with the approval of the people, and enforced by the magistrates.

But the people, the adult male citizens of Rome, could also pass laws, without reference to the senate, and they elected ten annual magistrates of their own. These 'tribunes of the people', originally appointed to make sure that the interests of the people were not threatened by any proposal discussed in the senate, constantly sat in the senate for this purpose, and it is not surprising that they came to be regarded as members of the senate themselves. It is easy to see how the various partners in the constitution depended on each other.

There was also another office, the dictatorship. On rare occasions, when a major crisis threatened, a dictator was appointed. He could hold office for as long as the emergency lasted, but in no circumstances for more than six months. His powers were supreme, and over-rode those of all other magistrates: he had an assistant, known as a *magister equitum* (master of the horse), who could represent him, but did not share his powers.

Troubled times affected the republic when the balance between the various parts of the state began to break down. One reason was that the members of the senate had won by far the largest share of Rome's new wealth. Their riches and the prestige that came from military command or provincial government made the senators arrogant and over-powerful. Their dominance was successfully challenged by tribunes in 133 and 123 BC, though each challenge cost the tribune his life. But the people had reasserted their power to pass laws without reference to the senate.

Another reason was that the organisation of a small city republic was no longer adequate for the management of a large empire. There was no civil service, with trained officials. Nor were there professionally trained officers to command the armies: the consuls and praetors, who both governed the provinces and commanded the armies, were amateurs. Furthermore, the army had, by 100 BC, developed from a part-time militia, conscripted in emergencies, into a permanent force of full-time soldiers, though this was a fact that the senate seemed unwilling to acknowledge. For it had taken no steps to provide regular pay or, perhaps more important, pensions for the soldiers. Consequently the men gave their loyalty, not to senate or state, but to their temporary commanders, who alone could arrange these benefits for them.

If one commander could persuade his troops to follow him and seize power, there was nothing to stop him, except another commander backed by another part of the army. Such conflicts did arise, and civil wars tormented the last hundred years of the republic, till Julius Caesar defeated his great rival, Pompey, and at last overwhelmed all opposition. In February of 44 BC, Julius Caesar was, both as an extraordinary honour, and to cure the republic's ills, appointed dictator, not this time for six months, but for life. To sixty leading men this was too much: he seemed to have superseded the magistrates, dispensed with the senate, and to have bribed the people into acceptance. So, on the Ides of March, they killed him.

AFTER CAESAR

At once, it became clear that they had formed no plans for the future, as if they believed that, with Caesar gone, the former glories of the old republic would magically reappear. But they were wrong. The state *needed* a new form of government that was strong enough to change the constitution. Given time, it might have been possible for the senate to re-form itself, and to create a more successful government for the empire by bringing in representatives from all the provinces. The provinces might then have become equal partners in the empire, not mere sources of wealth for Roman officials and merchants to plunder. Given time, an efficient civil service might have been created. And a new army, sensibly recruited and cared for, with officers carefully selected and trained, might have learnt to give its loyalty not to an individual, but to the state.

But there was no time. Within months of Caesar's death a 'gang of three' seized power. This triumvirate was composed of Antony, Caesar's fellow consul, Lepidus, Caesar's *magister equitum*, and Octavian, Caesar's great-nephew. Caesar's will had revealed both that Octavian was his heir, and that he had been adopted as his son. Octavian was only eighteen, and physically weak, but intelligent and ruthless. Within a year Brutus and Cassius, defeated by Antony and Octavian in a great battle at Philippi in Greece, had committed suicide. By this time none of the other assassins was left alive.

The triumvirate divided the Roman world. Antony, the senior partner, took the east, with its adventurous prospects of fresh conquests. Lepidus was dismissed to Africa, where his influence swiftly decreased. Octavian received Italy and the western provinces, with the grim task of defeating the remaining forces opposed to the triumvirate, who had occupied Sicily and Sardinia, and of healing the wounds that Italy and Rome had suffered. He was slowly, and perhaps luckily, successful, and among other things, eliminated Lepidus. Antony meanwhile had fallen victim to the charms of Cleopatra, queen of Egypt, and was losing interest in Rome. When Antony divorced Octavian's sister, a clash was inevitable. In 31 BC Antony and Cleopatra were defeated by Octavian at Actium in Greece. They fled to Alexandria where they committed suicide.

AUGUSTUS

Peace at last. Octavian was left in sole command of the empire, just as Caesar had been fourteen years earlier. He now had the time, and the ability, to restructure the government: he also had the intelligence to understand that whatever changes he made, it must at least appear that the republic had been preserved – otherwise the assassins' knives would be sharpened for him too. One man must govern Rome and command the armies, but the dignity of the ex-governors and ex-commanders, the senators, must be respected. A master-stroke of propaganda was needed, and achieved.

On the Ides of January, 27 BC, to quote Octavian's own words, 'At a time when I was, as everyone admitted, in complete command of affairs, I transferred the republic from my power to the control of the senate and people of Rome.' There was an uproar from those senators who had not been forewarned. But Octavian had not abdicated without making other careful arrangements. He had kept the consulship. And he modestly allowed himself to be persuaded by the appeals of the senate to take over, for ten years, a province of Spain, Gaul and Syria combined – and with command of most of the army. Three days later he was given the title of 'Augustus', by which he has been known ever after, an honour which set him apart from his contemporaries. He could say, and in theory he was right, 'After this time I had no more official power than the other men who were my colleagues in the various magistracies, though I did excel them all in prestige.' Augustus was no more than *primus inter pares*, first among equals. Though this was was not the whole truth, the fiction was happily accepted by the Romans, for the alternative was civil war, and that was unthinkable. And they were happy to call him 'princeps': *princeps senatus*, leader of the senate, was a republican title to which they had long been accustomed, and this simple word *princeps* seemed to fit Augustus' new position very well. (However, the subtlety of the word was soon lost, and his successors were called emperors – that word, derived from *imperator*, 'army commander', indicated their real position.) Later Augustus also assumed tribunician powers – his noble birth prevented him from actually being a tribune – which he liked to emphasise, as symbolising his position as protector of the people.

So in 27 BC the principate[5] began. It was to last, with changes, for the next five hundred years in Rome, and in Constantinople till AD 1453. And it was the history of the principate that, at some time after AD 100, Tacitus set out to record. Or rather it was its decline under successive emperors that interested him. Though the beginning under Augustus may have been promising, his successors were, Tacitus believed, so corrupted by their power that they turned into selfish monsters. Moreover, their fears that others might be tempted to deprive them of their enviable position made them suspicious, and their suspicions made them cruel.

TACITUS – SENATOR AND HISTORIAN

Tacitus was probably born in AD 55. He followed a conventional political career. After service in the army as a junior officer, he was appointed to a minor adminstrative post. Election to the quaestorship, which brought him into the senate, and the praetorship followed in due course. He had had the good fortune to marry the daughter of Agricola, the most famous of the governors of Roman Britain, and was himself appointed to the governorship of a minor province in AD 90. On his return in AD 93 he found Rome suffering under a reign of terror imposed by Domitian, one of Rome's cruellest emperors. For three years Tacitus sat in the senate in fear of his life. He was forced to join in congratulations, couched in terms of sickening flattery, which were offered to Domitian when he escaped some real or imagined plot against his life. He was forced to thank him for ridding the state, by ruthless execution, of those who had conspired against him, even though these were Tacitus' friends and fellow senators. Tacitus never forgot his own humiliation and shame. Though he was writing under Trajan, an enlightened and benevolent emperor, who even encouraged free speech, Tacitus never forgot the horrors he had witnessed, and never forgot that to some extent the blame for them belonged to Augustus, for it was he who had set up the system which had made such horrors possible.

Tacitus was also saddened by realising that there was no practical alternative to rule by emperors. In order to rule, the emperors had to have power, which could hardly be limited; and power corrupted. Tacitus illustrates his gloomy convictions in the story of a man called Arruntius, who had been accused of treason in the reign of Tiberius. Arruntius preferred suicide to execution, and was intent on taking his own life. His friends knew that the emperor Tiberius was dying, and begged him to delay. He refused. 'I can survive the few days till Tiberius dies, but how can I avoid the young emperor who will follow him? Tiberius was a man of experience, but he was still corrupted and changed by absolute power. Will Gaius, hardly adult yet, and completely inexperienced, be any better? I see even crueller times ahead. I am escaping the past, and the future.' With this prophecy he opened his veins.

So Tacitus wrote with a moral purpose. He wanted to expose the evils of the principate, in the hope that men might learn to recognise them in the future, and so, perhaps, escape them. 'I believe', he wrote, 'that the duty of history is to record what is good, and to make whatever is evil, in word or deed, afraid of the condemnation of posterity.'

We now believe that much of Tacitus' despair was unjustified. Life in the provinces of the empire, for example, was hardly affected by the excesses of even the worst emperors. The drama of his history largely happened in Rome, in the emperors' court, and it is on this that he concentrates, his vision distorted by his own experiences. He hardly spares a glance for the fortunes of the vast majority of the emperors' subjects. There is a contradiction, too, to be seen in what Tacitus writes: his descriptions of Tiberius' cruelties often illustrate the benefits of his rule.

Although, as a senator, Tacitus could refer to the Public Record Office, he will have been denied access to imperial archives. He had to rely on earlier historians, some obviously supporting imperial rule, others, less obviously, opposing it. Though he rarely quotes them directly, their influence can be seen in the differing motives which are often put forward for an emperor's actions. Tacitus will not state what he thinks is the true motive, but simply by constantly quoting the malicious view, he succeeds in darkening the picture. He is not quite so free from bias as he claims.

However, Tacitus' account of the period as a whole is a magnificent work, vivid and searching. The period itself is of high importance: this was the summit of a great empire, the only time in the world's history when the whole Mediterranean region was under one rule. We are indebted to the *Annals*, the name by which Tacitus' history is known, for most of our understanding and knowledge of these years, for it is the only full and connected history that has survived. Though we may dispute the historian's judgement, the facts he mentions, whenever they can be checked by other literary or archaeological evidence, prove remarkably accurate, and the depth and variety of his story is without parallel. The style is no less remarkable. The Latin in which it is written is very dense and difficult, full of colourful phrases and incisive epigrams, whose flavour is impossible to capture in English.

Another problem for the translator lies in the nature of the history. 'Annals' are the annual record of events. For each year Tacitus will record what happened in the court, in the rest of Rome, in Italy and the provinces. Only rarely will he give a continuous report of events in one region that extend over more than one year, though he does recount Boudica's revolt in one passage. So some topics will appear disjointed, even when the various parts are assembled in one chapter, as they are, for example, in 'Treason'. The repetition of Roman names can also be confusing: perhaps the following will be helpful when you read about them later. Tiberius had a brother named Drusus, who appears in Chapter 1. Tiberius's son, named Drusus after his uncle, appears in Chapters 2 and 3. Tiberius' nephew Germanicus also had a son named Drusus, and he too appears in Chapter 3. The Agrippina who appears in Chapters 7 and 8 is the daughter of the Agrippina who appears in the earlier chapters as Germanicus' wife. The real name of Tiberius' daughter-in-law Livilla was Livia, but she is called Livilla in Chapter 3 to distinguish her from Tiberius' mother.

The following tables may be helpful.

Table of dates

59 BC	Julius Caesar elected consul, forms an alliance with Pompey and Crassus, which dominates Rome.
53	Crassus killed in war which he had started against Parthia.
49	Caesar crosses the river Rubicon, in N. Italy, and so starts civil war.
48	Pompey killed in Egypt, after defeat by Caesar at Pharsalus in Greece.
44	Caesar assassinated by Brutus, Cassius and others. Antony, Lepidus and Octavian form a triumvirate.
42	Brutus and Cassius, defeated at Philippi in Greece, commit suicide.
36	Pompey's son defeated by Octavian in Sicily.
31	Antony and Clepatra beaten at Actium in Greece.
30	Antony and Cleopatra take their own lives at Alexandria.
27	Octavian 'restores the republic' and is awarded the title of AUGUSTUS.
23	Augustus gives up the consulship, and assumes tribunician powers.
AD 14	TIBERIUS succeeds Augustus. Sejanus becomes Praetorian Prefect.
23	Tiberius's son Drusus dies.
26	Tiberius leaves Rome for Capri.
31	Sejanus executed.
33	Agrippina starved to death.
37	GAIUS Caligula succeeds Tiberius. The future emperor Nero is born.
41	CLAUDIUS hailed as emperor by the Praetorian Guard.
43	Invasion of Britain.
49	Claudius marries Agrippina.
54	NERO succeeds Claudius.
55	Tacitus born.
59	Agrippina murdered.
60	Revolt of Boudica.
64	Great Fire of Rome.
68	Nero commits suicide. GALBA succeeds.
69	Year of the Four Emperors, GALBA, OTHO, VITELLIUS, VESPASIAN.
79	TITUS succeeds his father Vespasian.
81	DOMITIAN succeeds his brother Titus.
88	Tacitus praetor.
89–93	Tacitus absent from Rome.
96	NERVA succeeds Domitian.
97	Tacitus consul.
98	TRAJAN succeeds Nerva.

The books of the Annals

Bk 1	AD 14–15 Augustus and Tiberius
Bk 2	AD 16–19
Bk 3	AD 20–2
Bk 4	AD 23–8
Bk 5	Only a few chapters from the beginning of AD 29: the rest is missing.
Bk 6	AD 31–7
Bks 7–10 missing	
Bk 11	AD 47–8 Claudius
Bk 12	AD 49–54
Bk 13	AD 54 end–58 Nero
Bk 14	AD 59–62
Bk 15	AD 63–5
Bk 16	AD 65–6
Bks 17–18 missing.	

The Roman emperors

Augustus	31 BC–AD 14
Tiberius	AD 14–37
Gaius	AD 37–41
Claudius	AD 41–54
Nero	AD 54–68
Galba	AD 68–9
Otho	AD 69
Vitellius	AD 69
Vespasian	AD 69–79
Titus	AD 79–81
Domitian	AD 81–96
Nerva	AD 96–8
Trajan	AD 98–117

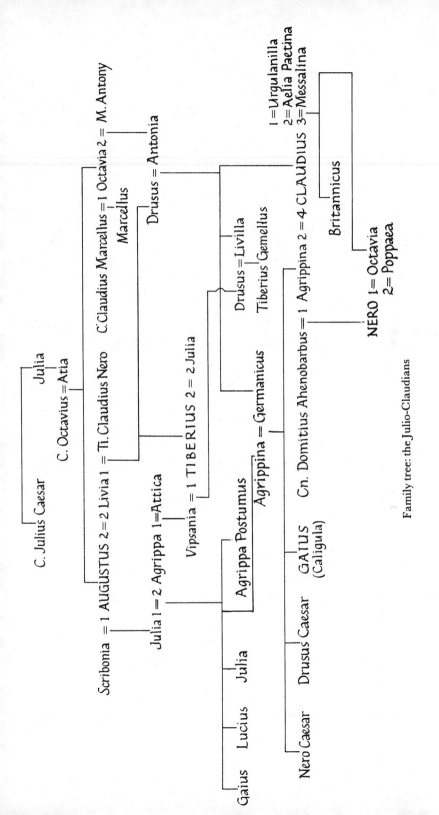

Family tree: the Julio-Claudians

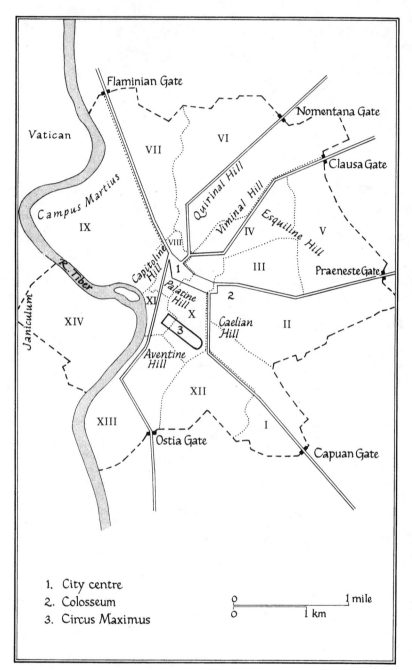

Imperial Rome

1 Augustus

Tacitus begins his history by explaining how he chose the starting point for his account.

The early history of Rome, with all its successes and failures, has been recorded by famous writers; and there was no lack of gifted men to describe the times of Augustus, till they were discouraged by seeing that flattery had more success than honesty. The histories written when Tiberius, Gaius, Claudius and Nero were still alive were distorted by fear, and those composed after their deaths were affected by hatred undimmed by time. That is why I have decided to deal briefly first with Augustus, especially with the end of his reign, and then with the times of Tiberius and his successors. I have no reason to be influenced by anger or bias, so they will not appear in my account.

A summary of Augustus' early years follows this passage. It begins with the defeat of Caesar's assassins at Philippi, and goes down to 27 BC, when he 'restored the republic' and received the title of Augustus, and then on to 23 BC, when he assumed the powers of a tribune.

No republican armies were left after the deaths of Brutus and Cassius; Pompey's son was defeated in Sicily, Lepidus was discarded and Antony killed. Octavius emerged without a rival as the only possible leader: he gave up the title of triumvir, boasting that he was merely consul, and satisfied that he could protect the people with his tribunician powers. He won over the army with gifts of money, the people of Rome with cheap subsidised food, and everyone in the empire with the delights of peace. Augustus' power grew steadily as he himself took over the functions of the senate, the state officials and the laws. War and political murder had removed even the bravest opposition. Of the surviving aristocracy, the first to accept their servility were the first to be rewarded with wealth and promotion. They did well out of the change, and preferred the new regime to the dangerous times that had preceded it. The provinces were equally satisfied: the rivalry of powerful men and the greed of

15

officials had caused them to distrust the senate and people of Rome. They had found no help in the laws, which were continually foiled by force or intrigue, or, in the last resort, by bribery.

> Augustus' next step was to make sure that he had an obvious successor, otherwise there might be attempts to overthrow him. Also if it was not quite clear who was to take his place when he died, civil war would be inevitable as rivals fought for the throne. He could not openly behave like a king and claim that his successor must be a member of the 'royal family', for this would deeply offend the leading families of what was still, in theory, a republic. However, he was able indirectly to indicate the men he wanted to succeed him at different points in his long reign. The fact that he had no son of his own, only a daughter, Julia, was an added complication.

To strengthen his dominant position, Augustus promoted his sister's son Marcellus, despite his youth, to a priesthood and an important administrative post. Marcus Agrippa, a man of humble birth but a splendid soldier who had helped win Augustus' battles for him, was honoured by successive consulships. Julia became the wife first of Marcellus, and then, when Marcellus died, of Agrippa. Tiberius and Drusus, sons of Augustus' wife Livia by her previous marriage, were distinguished by the title 'General'. Augustus' own line produced heirs too, for Gaius and Lucius, the sons of Julia and Agrippa, were adopted into his own family... After Agrippa died both Lucius and Gaius met with early but natural deaths, unless their stepmother Livia had a hand in them: Lucius was on his way to join the armies in Spain, Gaius was returning in poor health from Armenia, where he had been wounded. Of Augustus' stepsons, Drusus had died in the previous year, and only Tiberius was left: everything was pointing at him. He was Augustus' adopted son, sharing both his military and his civil authority, and had visited all the armies. (This was due, not, as before, to his mother's underhand scheming, but to her open request: she had complete control over the aging Augustus...). Yet it was Tiberius' nephew, Germanicus, who was appointed to the command of the eight legions[6] on the Rhine, and Augustus instructed Tiberius, even though he had a young son of his own, to adopt Germanicus: he had to make quite certain that there was someone to succeed him.

16

At this time [AD 14] there was peace throughout the empire, except for the war still being fought against the Germans. This was intended to wipe out the disgrace suffered when Quinctilius Varus'[7] army was lost – there was no wish to extend the empire or to exact booty in compensation. The city of Rome was free from unrest, the titles of the officers of state were unchanged. The men now in their prime had been born after the victory at Actium, and most older men in the civil war preceding it. Very few had any memory of republican government.

It was, in fact, the very length of Augustus' reign – nearly forty-five years – that perhaps did more than anything to ensure that the change from republic to principate was easy and successful.

The death of Augustus

The transformation of the state was complete, the good old ways were gone for ever. Political equality had disappeared, and everyone waited on the command of the emperor. This had caused no immediate anxiety as long as Augustus was fit and well and in full control of himself, his family and imperial affairs. But now he was approaching eighty and worn out by illness: as his end came near there were hopes of some change. A few men talked uselessly of the benefits of liberty, many were afraid of war, some even wanted it. The majority gossiped disparagingly about possible successors . . .

While rumours flourished, Augustus' health deteriorated, and there was even some suspicion that Livia was responsible . . . Whatever the truth may be, Tiberius was summoned by an urgent letter from his mother. Whether Augustus was still alive when Tiberius reached Nola,[8] or already dead, cannot now be established: Livia had posted sentries to seal off the house and surrounding streets, and from time to time hopeful bulletins were issued. But as soon as the necessary precautions had been taken, it was announced simultaneously that Augustus' life was over and that Tiberius was in command . . .

At Rome, consuls, senators and knights rushed headlong into servitude. The most prominent men showed the least sincerity or restraint – their features were carefully arranged to avoid showing pleasure at the departure of one emperor or gloom at the arrival of another, combining tears and joy, condolence and flattery. The oath of loyalty to Tiberius was taken first by the

consuls Pompeius and Appuleius; next, in their presence, by
Strabo, commander of the Praetorian Guard,[9] and Turranius,
Controller of the Corn Supply; then by the senate, army and
people. Tiberius initiated all business through the consuls, as
though the republic was still alive and as if he himself were
unsure of becoming emperor. Even the summons to a meeting
was issued to the senators only by virtue of the tribunician power
given him by Augustus. It was short and simple: he would
arrange about the honours to be paid to his father, but in the
mean time would not leave the body – this was the only business
of state he would undertake.

However, as soon as Augustus had died, Tiberius had given
the password to the Praetorian Guard, as if he were already their
commander-in-chief. He had an official armed bodyguard, and
soldiers escorted him on his visits to the forum and senate house.
He sent intructions to the army as though he was already
emperor – the only hesitation he showed was in addressing the
senate. The main reason for this was his anxiety that
Germanicus, who commanded huge forces of legions and
auxiliaries,[10] and who was extremely popular with the people,
might choose to seize the throne rather than wait for it. It would
look better if it seemed that Tiberius had been chosen and
summoned by popular feeling, and had not crept into power
through his mother's schemes and adoption by a senile
stepfather.

> Tacitus' criticism of Tiberius for assuming power is quite
> unjustified, for *someone* had to take control of the state, and
> Tiberius was the obvious person to do so, as Augustus had
> intended. Tacitus proceeds with a description of Augustus'
> funeral, and then goes on to compare some contemporary
> accounts of his career, some highly favourable, others strongly
> critical. Then he reverts to the events of the first few weeks of
> Tiberius' rule.

Augustus was buried in traditional fashion: it was decreed that a
temple should be built to him, and that he should be treated as a
god. Then prayers were directed towards Tiberius. He made
various statements about the greatness of the empire, and his
own diffidence. Only a character like the great Augustus, he said,
had been equal to such a task. He had discovered for himself,
when invited to share the responsibilities of government, how
hard and unpredictable was the burden of absolute power. In a

state that could rely on many distinguished citizens, everything should not be entrusted to one man: the administration of the state could more easily be effected by the joint efforts of a larger number.

There was more show than credibility in such remarks. Moreover Tiberius' words, either by habit or nature, were always hesitant and obscure, even when he was not hiding anything: but now that he was trying to conceal his real feelings he became even more cryptic and hard to understand. The senators knew well enough what was in his mind – their real concern was to conceal the fact, so they poured out a flood of entreaties accompanied by tears and lamentation, stretching their hands to the heavens above, towards the statue of Augustus, and to Tiberius himself.

At this point Tiberius ordered a document to be produced and read aloud. It contained a list of the state's resources, the number of Roman and allied troops in the various armies, and details of the fleets: it also covered the dependent kingdoms, provinces, direct and indirect taxation, essential expenditure and grants. Augustus had written this out in his own hand; he had added the advice that the empire should not be extended beyond its existing frontiers – Augustus was either afraid of the future, or jealous of someone else's success.

The senate sank to the most abject entreaties. Tiberius casually remarked that though he could not cope with the whole state he would undertake any part of it entrusted to him. At this Asinius Gallus said, 'Then tell us, Caesar, which part do you want?' Tiberius was taken aback by the unexpected question and for a moment said nothing. Then collecting his thoughts, he replied that it was not reasonable to expect him to choose or reject any one part, when he preferred to be excused the whole lot. Gallus guessed from Tiberius' expression that he was offended, and spoke again: his intention in asking the question had not been to split up what could not be divided, but to make Tiberius himself admit that the state was one single body needing a single mind to control it. He went on to praise Augustus and to remind Tiberius of his long and splendid service both as soldier and civilian, but even so could not soothe the emperor's anger.

At last Tiberius gradually gave in: he was worn down by their united outcry and individual appeals. He did not actually admit that he was accepting the throne, but he did stop saying no to the senate's repeated requests.

2 Mutiny

Once he had assumed power as emperor, in AD 14, Tiberius did not have to wait long for trouble to start: he was soon faced with the burdens of 'absolute power' which he had appeared so anxious to avoid. However the trouble did not come from senate or people, who were thoroughly cowed, but from troops in the Roman provinces.

This was the situation in Rome when a mutiny broke out among the legions in Pannonia. It was not that conditions had altered; the troops merely thought that the change of emperor offered the chance of uncontrolled rioting and the hope of some profit to be made from a civil war. Three legions were sharing a summer camp under the command of Junius Blaesus. When he heard of Augustus' death and the accession of Tiberius, he suspended normal duties for mourning for the former, or rejoicing for the latter. The soldiers' boisterous games turned to squabbling, and they listened to every trouble-maker who held forth. In the end, rejecting discipline and work, they thought only of idleness and a comfortable life.

There was in the camp a common soldier called Pescennius who had been a cheer-leader in the theatre: he had a ready tongue, experienced in arousing applause for the actors who hired him. He started working on the minds of the soldiers: they were ignorant men, worried about their terms of service under a new emperor. Under the cover of twilight or darkness, when the steadier troops had dispersed to their tents, he gathered the riff-raff together. Finding among them some associates prepared to start a mutiny, Pescennius delivered a sort of official speech.

'Why do we behave like slaves, obeying a few centurions[11] and half a dozen officers? Now's the time to pluck up courage and ask for better conditions, when we can aim our prayers – or weapons – at an emperor who is still new and unsure of himself. We've done nothing for years, and suffered for it. Some of us are old men, with thirty or forty years' service, with bodies disabled by wounds. Even when we are discharged, we still have to go on serving in the veterans' section – the same hard work under a different name. Anyone who survives all the risks is dumped in some remote country where he gets some watery swamp or barren mountain for his "farm".[12]

'A soldier's life is hard, and underpaid! Body and soul for a few coppers a day! And out of that we have to pay for clothes, weapons and tents, and bribe the centurions if we don't want to be beaten, or have endless duties. There's never any rest from blows or wounds, bitter winters or summer exercises, bloody wars or dreary peace! Our only chance of improvement is military service by contract – double pay, sixteen years' service and no extra time in the "reserves", gratuities paid in cash and in camp. The Praetorians get four times our pay, and after sixteen years they're discharged to their homes, and there's no more danger in their jobs than ours. I'm not saying anything against sentry duty in Rome, but we're on guard against real savages, right under our noses!'

Bursts of rowdy applause accompanied his words, and at appropriate times the men pointed indignantly at the scars left by the lash, their grey hairs, and the bare flesh showing through their tattered clothes.

> For a short time Blaesus, the commander, managed to calm them down. But some troops who had been away, building roads and bridges, started looting local villages when they heard of the mutiny, and hurried back to camp.

Their arrival renewed the mutiny, and men began to wander off to plunder the neighbourhood. There were a few with excessive loads of booty: Blaesus had them whipped and thrown into prison to discourage the others – for the centurions and the better soldiers were still obeying orders. But as the looters were being dragged off they resisted, grabbing the legs of the bystanders. Shouting the names of their friends and calling on their century, cohort or legion, they cried that the same fate awaited everyone. They hurled abuse at Blaesus and called on the gods for help, doing everything to stir up indignation, sympathy, fear and anger. The prison was broken open as men rushed to their rescue, and deserters and condemned murderers were unchained and joined the mob.

More agitation

> The following incident included by Tacitus illustrates how ordinary people, caught up in violent events, can be manipulated by agitators for their own ends.

The disorder grew worse, and more and more ring-leaders appeared. A soldier called Vibulenus was hoisted on the shoulders of some men grouped in front of Blaesus' platform. As the mutineers watched to see what he would do he cried, 'You've saved those poor innocent men, but who can give my brother back his life, or give him back to me? The army in Germany sent him here to discuss our common interests. But last night Blaesus had my brother's throat cut by the gladiators he keeps under arms to kill off us soldiers. Where are you hiding his body, general? Even the enemy let us bury our dead. You can have me butchered too, when I've paid him my last farewell; then let us both be buried. We've done nothing wrong, only what's best for the troops.'

Vibulenus increased the effect of his words by weeping, and striking his face and chest with his hands. Then he pushed aside those who were holding him and threw himself headlong at the feet of man after man. He aroused such fury and hatred among the soldiers that one group of them arrested the gladiators – they were Blaesus' slaves – another the rest of his servants, and a third group rushed off to look for the body. But they quickly discovered that there was no body to be found, that the slaves denied even under torture that anyone had been killed, and that Vibulenus had never even had a brother. They were very close to killing Blaesus when they learnt the truth. But they did hustle the officers and camp commandant out of the gates, pilfering their luggage, and actually killed the centurion Lucilius. He was jokingly nicknamed 'Gimme another', for whenever he broke his cane over a soldier's back he used to call loudly for another, and then another.

Drusus reaches the Danube

When news of the mutiny reached Rome, Tiberius sent his son Drusus, with some distinguished advisers and two cohorts of the Praetorian Guard, to see what could be done.

The legions came to meet Drusus as he approached, apparently as a mark of respect – but there were no demonstrations of welcome, no parade of medals or decorations. The men were appallingly filthy, and the look on their faces, intended to show sorrow, was closer to insolence. As soon as Drusus had passed the outer defences, sentries were posted at the gates, and armed detachments occupied key places in the camp. The remainder

22

flocked round the general's platform in a huge throng. Drusus stood there and raised his hand for silence. Every time the mutineers surveyed their own great numbers they yelled defiance, but lost confidence when they looked again at the prince – uncertain mutterings were followed by a fierce roar, then sudden quiet. Alternating looks of hostility and alarm reflected their changing emotions.

At last, when the noise abated, Drusus read out a letter from his father. His bravest legions, it said, with whom Tiberius had endured so many campaigns, were his especial concern. As soon as he had recovered from his bereavement, he would submit their demands to the senate. Meanwhile he had sent his son to grant, without delay, whatever immediate concessions could be made. Everything else would have to wait for the senate, which was entitled to a share in granting or refusing their requests.

The soldiers replied that Julius Clemens, the centurion, would speak for them. He proposed discharge after sixteen years, cash gratuities on completion of service, pay of a denarius[13] a day, and abolition of veteran service. These were matters, said Drusus, for the senate and emperor to decide. The soldiers roared their anger:

'What is the point of coming here if you haven't been given powers to increase our pay or improve our conditions, if in fact you can't do anything for us? Anyone else is allowed to have us flogged or put to death. Tiberius used to frustrate our requests by referring them to Augustus, and now you're using the same tactics. Are we only going to see powerless youngsters? It's extraordinary that the emperor only refers army reforms to the senate – he ought to consult them about the death penalty and fighting as well! He can give punishment when he likes, does he have to have permission for rewards?'

They moved away from the platform, but if they met a Praetorian Guardsman or one of Drusus' advisers they made threatening gestures, looking for an excuse to start arguing or fighting... It looked as if some dreadful crime might be committed at nightfall, but a stroke of luck prevented it: the light of the moon suddenly began to fade. Unaware of the true explanation of the eclipse, the soldiers took it as an omen of their present situation. The failure of the light was like the failure of their own efforts, and they thought that success would come only if the moon's light could be encouraged to return. So they clashed bronze pans together, and blew loud blasts on their trumpets and horns. If the light seemed stronger they rejoiced, if dimmer they despaired: finally clouds came across the face of the moon and hid it from sight altogether. It appeared to them to be buried in darkness. If mens' minds are ever unbalanced they are ready to believe any superstition; so now they wailed that the gods were appalled by their crimes and that everlasting hardships would be their reward.

Drusus quells the mutiny

Drusus was quick to seize the opportunity offered by the soldiers' loss of confidence; he sent Clemens and other decent officers round the camp, urging the men to give up the mutiny. Pescennius and Vibulenus, they said, were never going to replace Tiberius or Drusus, or produce the soldiers' pay – why listen to them? The mutineers wavered. Drusus addressed them in the morning, promising to recommend mercy if they returned to discipline. They agreed at once, and Blaesus' son was sent to Rome.

But Drusus was fond of tough measures. He ordered Vibulenus and Pescennius to be brought to him and killed. It was generally reported that they were buried inside his tent, though others say that their bodies were thrown outside the camp for all to see. Then a search was started for the chief ring-leaders, and some of them, as they straggled away outside the camp, were hacked down by the centurions and guardsmen; others were handed over by their own ex-comrades as a proof of loyalty.

The troubles of the soldiers were aggravated by an early winter: the rain was continuous and so hard that they could not leave their tents for a meeting; they had the greatest difficulty in preventing their standards[14] being carried away by the winds and floods. Dread of divine anger still hung over them: it was not by chance, they thought, that, in the face of their wickedness, planets were fading and tempests raged. There would be no relief from their plight unless they abandoned this ill-fated, polluted camp and returned to their own winter quarters, purged from guilt. First the Eighth Legion left, then the Fifteenth. The men of the Ninth had loudly insisted that they should wait for Tiberius' letter; but they had been isolated by the departure of the others, and so did voluntarily what would soon have been forced upon them. Drusus considered that the situation was now quiet enough, and went back to Rome without waiting for the return of the delegation.

Germanicus in Germany

At about the same time as Drusus was confronting the army in Pannonia, danger threatened in Germany as well. Here there were two armies guarding the Rhine frontier, one in north Germany, one in the south. It was the legions in the north that mutinied, for the same reasons as the troops in Pannonia.

News of his men's disloyalty brought Germanicus hurrying to them. The troops flocked round him in an undisciplined mass. He started his address by praising Augustus, then Tiberius' success in Germany in command of these same legions. Then he asked foolishly, 'Where's your soldierly bearing, where's your famous traditional discipline?' The men interrupted him, tearing off their clothes to show the scars left by wounds or flogging, and roared their complaints.

Some of them demanded the money bequeathed them by Augustus, and at the same time indicated their personal support for Germanicus: if he wanted the throne he could count on them. Germanicus leapt off the platform as if their criminal suggestion were some contagious disease. As he tried to get away, the soldiers barred his path with their swords, threatening to kill him if he did not climb back. But he shouted that death was better than dishonour, drew his sword, raised it to his breast and would have driven it into his heart if the men around him had not seized his right arm and forcibly restrained him. Some of the men pressing forward from the back and, though it is hard to believe, even a few individuals who had come right up to him, told him to strike. A soldier named Calusidius even offered him his own sword saying, 'This one's sharper!' Angry though the men were, this seemed too brutal and heartless, and there was time for his friends to hurry Germanicus off to his quarters.

There they discussed what they ought to do... After a long debate they decided to issue a letter in the name of Tiberius, promising full discharge to men who had served twenty years: men with sixteen years' service would be kept in the ranks, but excused all duties except beating off enemy attacks: the legacies they had demanded would be paid – but double the original amount!

The soldiers made the most of their position and demanded that the promises should be kept immediately. The money had to be scraped together out of the travelling expenses of Germanicus and his staff officers. But Germanicus' indecisive measures did not bring any major improvement. The same concessions had to be made to the army in south Germany, and discipline everywhere was precarious. A minor rebellion was put down with the execution of a couple of soldiers, but a senior officer had to run for his life in the disorder that followed. An embassy sent by the senate to console Germanicus on Augustus' death, and to confirm his command, was jeered at and its leader nearly murdered. Germanicus scolded his men, but had to send the delegation away under the protection of auxiliary troops.

The flight of Agrippina

During these grim days there was widespread criticism of Germanicus for not joining the army in south Germany, which was still loyal and might have suppressed the uprising. Grants of discharge and money and such soft measures, it was said, were mistakes, or worse. Germanicus might risk his own life, but should not keep his pregnant wife and their little son among crazy and criminal troops. He should send them back, for Tiberius' sake, and for Rome's. When his wife dismissed the suggestion and claimed that Augustus' grand-daughter could face any peril, Germanicus hesitated for a while, but then burst into tears, embraced his expectant wife and their son and persuaded her to depart.

The unhappy troop of women trudged away; a general's wife in flight, clasping her baby son in her arms; the sobbing wives of their friends dragging along with her. The husbands left behind were no less distressed. This was no triumphant Caesar in his camp – it looked more like a captured city. The sobs and groans attracted the attention of the soldiers. They piled out of their tents to ask the reason for this unhappy sound and gloomy sight. Noble ladies without a centurion or soldier to guard them, with nothing to mark the general's wife, no sign of the usual escort, were going for protection to the Treveri, a foreign tribe! The soldiers were stricken with shame and sorrow, remembering that she was the daughter of Agrippa, the grand-daughter of Augustus and daughter-in-law of Drusus. They recalled that she was the mother of six, a noble wife: her baby son had been born and brought up in camp, among the troops: they had nicknamed him 'Little Boots' (Caligula) because, to win their affection, he was dressed in miniature army-boots.

But the soldiers' jealousy of the Treveri affected them more than anything. Some blocked Agrippina's path, and begged her to come back and stay; most ran back to Germanicus – he was still bitter and angry as they crowded round him: 'I do not love my wife and son any more than my father or my country, but he is protected by his position and dignity, and the empire by its other armies. Though I would willingly sacrifice my wife and children for your glory, I am now taking them out of reach of your crazy hands. If any crime is to be committed, it must be my blood that pays for it – do not increase your guilt by murdering the grand-daughter of Augustus or slaying the daughter-in-law of Tiberius.'

> Germanicus went on in similar fashion, and finished by telling them to search out the culprits to prove their sorrow and loyalty. The whole theatrical scene and his dramatic words at last swung the soldiers round.

With a complete change of heart they ran off, tied up the ring-leaders and dragged them back before Caetronius, commander of the First Legion. They were tried and punished as follows. The soldiers stood in a pack, their swords ready; the officers paraded the prisoners one at a time on the platform – if the soldiers shouted 'Guilty', the man was thrown down and hacked to death. The soldiers revelled in the butchery as if they were washing away their guilt. Germanicus had not given the orders, but did nothing to stop them – any disgust at the atrocity would fall on their shoulders, not on his.

> However, the two legions which had started the mutiny still had to be dealt with. Germanicus was now prepared to use force, and collected auxiliaries to do so – he still could not trust the penitent legions.

Although Germanicus had assembled an army and was ready to punish the mutineers, he thought he should give them time to see if they would learn from recent events. He sent a letter to the commander, Caecina, to say that he was coming with a large army: unless the guilty men were punished before he reached them, he would execute the lot. Caecina secretly read out the letter to the standard-bearers [there were no centurions left] and any other loyal troops, and begged them to save their legions from disgrace and themselves from death ... They tested the feelings of men they thought reliable, and found that most of them were loyal. They fixed a time with Caecina to strike down the worst criminals and ring-leaders. When the signal was given, they burst into their tents, caught their victims unawares and butchered them. Only those in the know were aware why the killing had started, and how it would end.

Later Germanicus entered the camp: weeping bitterly he cried, 'This is not a cure, it's a disaster!' He ordered the bodies to be cremated.

Feelings at Rome

Tacitus records the emotions aroused in the capital by the news of the mutinies. Tiberius' attitude seems practical and sensible.

While Rome was still wondering what was happening in Pannonia, news of the German mutiny arrived. In a panic the citizens reproached Tiberius, saying that while he was making fools of the senate and people by pretending to be unsure of assuming power, the army was in rebellion. 'How', they protested, 'can two immature and inexperienced young men deal with it? He ought to have gone himself: faced by the majesty of their Commander-in-Chief, the troops would have backed down on seeing an experienced emperor, who alone has the power to make concessions as well as to punish. Augustus visited Germany often enough, when he was old and tired: why is Tiberius, in the prime of life, sitting in the senate and quibbling about their speeches? He has done enough to ensure that the citizens of Rome accept their slavery; now he ought to be persuading the soldiers to accept the peace.'

Tiberius was quite unmoved by such remarks. He was determined not to endanger himself or the nation by leaving the capital. He had many different things to worry about – the army in Germany was stronger, that in Pannonia was nearer; the former had the might of the Gallic province behind it, but the latter threatened Italy. Which should he deal with first? Would those placed second be offended? By using his sons, he could deal with both at the same time, without risking his own position – the more remote he was, the more awesome he would be. At the same time the young men would be excused if they had to refer to their father – any resistance to them could then be conciliated or crushed by himself – but if the emperor's own efforts were rejected, no course of action was left. However, as if he were on the point of setting out at any moment, Tiberius chose his staff, collected the baggage and equipped the ships. Then he pleaded bad weather or the pressure of business as an excuse – even shrewd men of affairs were deceived for a while; the man in the street was the next to realise the truth, the provincials last of all.

To distract his dissatisfied soldiers Germanicus had a bridge built over the Rhine and invaded Germany, devastating the country to a depth of fifty miles beyond the river. The morale of his men was vastly improved by a victory over a German army, and the past was forgotten.

But Tiberius was worried as well as pleased by the news – though glad that the mutiny was over, he was dismayed by Germanicus' grants of money and early discharge to win the goodwill of his troops, and by his military triumph. He reported Germanicus' achievements to the senate and spoke at length about his success. But his remarks were too flowery to be accepted as coming from the heart. The few words that he spoke in praise of Drusus for quelling the mutiny in Pannonia were much more sincere. All the concessions made by Germanicus were granted to the Pannonian army as well.

Germanicus – the final years

Little of AD 14 was left when Germanicus led his repentant legions to an easy victory over the unsuspecting Germans across the Rhine. In the winter he gained Tiberius' permission for ambitious operations on a far larger scale, and in AD 15 and 16 led Roman troops far into Germany. He even had one thousand ships built to transport his armies past the coasts of Belgium and Holland to the mouth of the River Ems. But his victories were far from complete, and the huge fleet was wrecked by bad weather on its journey home. Though Germanicus believed that only one more campaign was needed to complete the conquest of Germany, Tiberius had grave doubts; and the results of three years' hard fighting were poor reward for the enormous expense of men and money. Germanicus was recalled to Rome, where he was awarded a splendid triumph to soften his disappointment.

Germanicus was immediately despatched again to take up a new command over all the eastern provinces. At the same time Calpurnius Piso was appointed governor of Syria, ostensibly to give Germanicus advice and assistance – his real mission was to keep a watchful eye on the young prince. Germanicus made a holiday of the journey out, calling at Athens and the site of ancient Troy. Every city greeted him and his family with processions and festivities; coins were struck in his honour, and two towns in Asia Minor were renamed after him to celebrate his visit: he was enormously popular. His main tasks – of reorganising the provinces on the eastern fringes of the empire, and installing a new king in Armenia – were soon and successfully completed.

In AD 19 Germanicus seriously offended Tiberius by a holiday visit to Egypt. No senators were allowed even to set foot in Egypt; it was so vital for Rome's corn supply that any potential rival to the emperor who gained control of its ports could threaten the emperor's security. Then Germanicus infuriated Tiberius even more, by issuing coins stamped with his own head, and by courting popularity with grants of cheap corn to the citizens of Alexandria.

On his return to Syria, Germanicus' dislike of the suspicious Piso reached such a point that he ordered Piso to leave the province. But soon Germanicus fell mysteriously ill and before long died, convinced that Piso had poisoned him. Piso unwisely tried to re-enter Syria, but was rejected. On his return to Rome he was prosecuted in the senate, but committed suicide before the trial was over, protesting his innocence and his loyalty to Tiberius. Nothing could persuade Agrippina, Germanicus' widow, that Tiberius had not contrived her husband's death, through Piso's agency. Tacitus clearly shared her suspicions.

3   Sejanus

During the last centuries of the republic it was customary for army generals to have a bodyguard, or *cohors praetoria*. Following this example, Augustus created for himself a permanent Praetorian Guard, though his consisted of nine cohorts, each of probably one thousand men. Three of these cohorts were billeted at various places in Rome itself, while the other six were in nearby towns. Augustus commanded the Guard himself until 2 BC when he appointed two Praetorian Prefects to take his place.

At the beginning of Tiberius' reign the Praetorian Prefects were L. Seius Strabo and his son, usually known simply as Sejanus. When his father was appointed governor of Egypt a year or two later, Sejanus was left in sole command. Sejanus was ambitious. By AD 23 he had concentrated all nine cohorts in Rome. From this time the Guard and its various commanders had great political importance, and sometimes considerable influence over the emperor. Sejanus was the first to demonstrate such power: Tacitus takes an almost grim delight in recounting Sejanus' evil influence, though admitting that, until AD 23, Tiberius' rule had been stable and prosperous.

Suddenly Fortune began to upset everything; Tiberius became cruel, or gave power to cruel men. Sejanus was the cause and beginning of the change. I shall describe his origins and character, and his criminal attempt to seize power. He was born at Vulsinii:[15] his father Seius Strabo was a Roman knight. As a young man Sejanus had become a friend of Augustus' grandson Gaius, and later won the affections of Tiberius so completely that the emperor, who was always obscure to others, would speak openly and frankly to him alone. This was due not to any cunning on the part of Sejanus (for in this the emperor easily outclassed him) but rather to the anger of the gods against Rome, for whose fortunes Sejanus' rise and fall were equally ruinous. He combined great courage with physical endurance, and was quick to blame others, or excuse himself. He was both obsequious and haughty, on the surface calm and modest, while inwardly enormously ambitious. Sometimes this made him extravagantly generous, more often it drove him to incessant hard work: which is just as dangerous, when the work is aimed at seizing the throne.

Formerly the power of the Praetorian Prefects had been small, but Sejanus increased it by concentrating the cohorts, previously scattered throughout Rome, into one barracks: thus orders could reach them all without delay, and the sight of their own strength and numbers would inspire confidence in themselves and terror in others. Sejanus's excuse was that his men became demoralised when they were kept apart, that in an emergency their services would be more effective, and that their discipline would improve if they were separated from the temptations of the city. When the barracks was built he gradually won popularity by spending time with the men, and addressing them personally by their names. He himself selected the centurions and officers. He curried favour with the senators, as well as with the soldiers, by bestowing high office or provincial commands on his supporters. He could not have done this without Tiberius, who went so far as to call him 'Partner of my labours', not only in casual conversation but also in the senate and popular assembly. Tiberius also let special honours be paid to the statues of Sejanus which stood in the theatres, town-centres and legionary headquarters.

The attack on the emperor's son

However, Sejanus' ambitions were blocked by the numerous heirs in the imperial family: Tiberius had a son, now thirty-five years old, and grown-up grandchildren. It would be dangerous to make a clean sweep of them all at once, while more subtle methods would take time. None the less he chose to act by stealth, beginning with Tiberius' son Drusus. Sejanus had cause for resentment: Drusus could not stand a rival, and losing his temper in some chance quarrel, raised his hand against Sejanus, and struck him in the face when he defended himself. After weighing all the possibilities, Sejanus decided the best course was to get at Drusus through his wife Livilla. She was Germanicus' sister, and though she had been an unattractive girl had grown into an outstanding beauty. Sejanus acted as if he were passionately in love, and seduced her. After this first success – for a woman who has lost her virtue will not say no to anything else – he egged her on with the hope of marriage to himself, a share in the throne and the death of her husband. And so a lady closely related to Augustus and Tiberius, the mother of Drusus' children, disgraced herself and her family, past and future, with a small-town lover, and gave up a life of certain honour and success for one of shame and uncertainty.

Whether Drusus suspected his wife or not, he certainly suspected Sejanus' ambition, and did not try to conceal his hatred.

So Sejanus decided that no time must be lost: he chose a slow-acting poison whose effects would look like a natural illness. It was given to Drusus by the eunuch Lygdus, as was discovered eight years later. Throughout his son's illness Tiberius continued to go into the senate, either because he was genuinely unworried, or perhaps to display his strength of character. He did not stop even when Drusus had died and was lying unburied. When, as a sign of their mourning, the consuls sat on the ordinary benches, Tiberius reminded them of their dignity and proper place. When the senators burst into tears, he comforted them with a speech unbroken by any sign of his own grief. He was aware, he said, that he was open to criticism for appearing in the senate after so recent a loss: most mourners could scarcely listen to their relatives, or bear the light of day, but that did not mean that they were weaklings. But he preferred to find a sterner comfort in the press of state affairs.

Germanicus' family

Tiberius went on to say that Nero and Drusus, the sons of Germanicus, were his only comfort, and commended them to the senate's care. In fact Tiberius disliked the boys, and their mother Agrippina; she in turn made no secret of her hostility, because she believed that Tiberius had had her husband poisoned. She may well have tried to organize a conspiracy to overthrow Tiberius, though there is no evidence. But it is certain that she and her sons still enjoyed great popularity, and the boys seemed the obvious heirs to the throne.

Then Tiberius delivered a speech in the forum in praise of his son. The senators and people assumed attitudes and accents of grief – all quite insincere, for they were secretly glad that the fortunes of Germanicus' family were reviving. However, this new public approval, and Agrippina's ill-concealed ambitions, only hastened their ruin. For when Sejanus saw that Drusus' death was neither avenged by the emperor nor mourned by the people he was encouraged to further crimes. His first attempt had turned out well; next he considered how to get rid of Germanicus' sons now that their succession seemed certain. It was impossible to poison the boys and their mother, for the loyalty of their servants was unassailable – as was Agrippina's virtue. So Sejanus attacked Agrippina's arrogance. He worked on the long-standing hatred felt for her by the emperor's mother, and on the newly aroused guilty conscience of Livilla: he got these two women to tell Tiberius that Agrippina, spurred on by her pride in her children and her popularity with the people, was dreaming of taking over the throne ...

A setback for Sejanus

Although Agrippina resisted Sejanus' malice for a long time, and became the head of a party openly opposed to Tiberius, Sejanus was confident that he now had nothing to fear from her. With Drusus dead and Agrippina out-manoeuvred, his way ahead seemed open. Moreover, by AD 25, Livilla was becoming impatient for marriage, so Sejanus wrote to Tiberius asking permission to marry her. Tiberius refused.

Sejanus was alarmed, not now about his marriage, but on more serious grounds: he begged Tiberius to pay no attention to suspicion, common gossip or envious criticism. He was afraid that if he closed his door to the stream of visitors his influence would decline; and that if he let them in he would leave himself open to accusations of seeking popularity. Consequently he tried another tack, to persuade Tiberius to leave Rome for some more pleasant place to live in. Sejanus thought that there would be many advantages in this: he would control visits to the emperor; letters would have to be brought by soldiers and would thus pass through his hands; later, weakened by age and softened by retirement, Tiberius would be more ready to hand over the burden of government. Then Sejanus could reduce the number of his visitors and so lessen his unpopularity, and at the same time increase his real power by giving up the appearance of it. Increasingly, he found fault with the pressures of city life, the crowds and endless stream of visitors, praising instead a life of peace and isolation, in which, far from troublesome misunder-standing, Tiberius could concentrate on what was important.

More trouble for Agrippina

At the same time Sejanus renewed his attacks on Agrippina and her family. The historian Suetonius actually says that Tiberius,

The emperor's family had not yet recovered [from the death of Drusus] when the first moves were taken which were to lead to the downfall of Agrippina: her cousin Claudia Pulchra was accused by Domitius Afer. He had recently been praetor, without any particular distinction, and was ready to do anything to achieve promotion: he charged Claudia Pulchra with immoral behaviour and adultery, and with using poison and witchcraft against the emperor. Agrippina was always an impetuous woman, and she was now furious at the plight of her cousin. Hurrying in to Tiberius, she happened to find him sacrificing to Augustus, and indignantly rebuked him. 'How can you sacrifice to Augustus while making charges against his descendants? You won't find his divine spirit in dumb statues, but in me, his grand-daughter. I'm aware of the real danger and grieve for my plight. The charge against Pulchra is a mere blind; she's in trouble because she's my friend, that's the only reason' . . . Her words brought a rare retort from the normally inscrutable Tiberius: grasping her arm, he quoted a Greek verse; 'You are not wronged because you are not queen.' But Pulchra was condemned . . .

Agrippina's unrelenting anger made her physically ill. When Tiberius visited her she wept long and silently, then began to pour out a mixture of reproaches and requests. She begged him to relieve her loneliness and let her remarry: 'she was still young enough, and decent women could not find consolation outside marriage; there were plenty of men in Rome ready to take on Germanicus' wife and children'. But Tiberius could see the political dangers of her request. He left without giving an answer despite her insistence, unwilling to show either his annoyance or his fears. This incident is not recorded in any history: I found it in the memoirs of her daughter, the younger Agrippina, the mother of Nero, who left behind an account of her life and the misfortunes of her family.

But Sejanus made Agrippina's unhappy state even worse, with-out letting her see that he was involved. His agents pretended to be her friends, and warned her to avoid dining with the emperor, because he was plotting to poison her. She was incapable of pretending; she sat next to him in silence, a grim expression on her face, and left her food untouched. When Tiberius noticed – or perhaps someone told him – in order to test her more strictly, he praised some fruit that had been set on the table and passed it to her himself. Agrippina was all the more suspicious; without tasting it she handed it to the servants. Tiberius said nothing openly, but whispered to his mother that it was not surprising that he should treat her harshly when she implied that he was a poisoner.

Tiberius leaves Rome

Eventually Tiberius did succumb to the pressures of his position: he had, after all, made it clear in AD 14 that he was unwilling to accept the burden of government, and the twelve years of his reign had not been easy. Sejanus' persuasions helped to make up his mind, and in AD 26 he did leave Rome: he never returned to the city. An incident on the journey south helps to explain his dependence on Sejanus.

At this time, a dangerous accident to Tiberius increased empty gossip and made him put even more confidence in Sejanus' loyalty and friendship. They were dining at a villa, called The Cave, in a huge natural cavern. A sudden rock-fall at its entrance crushed several of the servants. There was a general panic and the emperor's fellow diners ran away. Sejanus crouched over Tiberius on hands and knees, shielding him from the falling boulders. That is how he was found by the soldiers who came to the rescue. His influence consequently became greater. Tiberius believed that he had no thought for himself, and followed his advice faithfully, even though it proved to be disastrous.

Tiberius retired to the island of Capri, which he rarely left. Sejanus returned to Rome as his agent, and was treated with almost more respect and awe than the emperor himself. In AD 28 Sejanus went to Capri for a long visit.

The senate were not worried about what happened on the frontiers, no matter how shameful it might be: it was the situation at home that terrified them. They tried to find some relief for their worries in flattery. Although the senate had met to discuss quite different matters, they now voted that altars should be built to Mercy and Friendship, and that on either side should be set statues of Tiberius and Sejanus. Again and again the senate asked for the chance to see them. But neither of them came to Rome or anywhere near it, thinking it good enough to leave the island and appear on the coast of Campania that faced it. So the senators went there, with the knights and many of the ordinary people, their eyes fixed anxiously on Sejanus. But to meet and talk to him was more difficult – only bribery, or collaboration in his schemes, opened his door. It became clear that his arrogance fed on the sight of such base and open servility. In Rome, scurrying crowds are to be seen every day, and the size of the city conceals what one man is doing. But there in Campania, queuing in the fields or on the shore, they had to put up with pompous and insolent doormen by day and by night. In the end, even this was forbidden. Anyone Sejanus had not chosen to see or talk to, hurried back to Rome overwhelmed with anxiety.

After Sejanus

At this point there is a gap in Tacitus' manuscript, and two years are missing. However, we know from other sources that Agrippina and her two eldest sons were exiled. Tiberius at last discovered what Sejanus' ambitions really were, and in AD 31 had him arrested and killed. Sejanus' divorced wife, Apicata, then revealed that Sejanus and Livilla had poisoned Tiberius' son Drusus: Livilla committed suicide. Embittered by grief and hatred, Tiberius took revenge on many of Sejanus' friends and supporters, who were executed, or forced to take their own lives. He even let his fury fall on Sejanus' children.

Popular anger was subsiding, and most people were satisfied with the previous executions, but a decision was now taken to punish the rest of Sejanus' children. They were taken to prison, the boy well aware of what was in store; the girl was so unsuspecting that she kept on asking what she had done wrong, and where she was being taken: 'I won't do it again! Why don't you smack me?' They were strangled, young as they were, and their bodies thrown down the Gemonian steps.[16]

Sejanus had been a treacherous and ruthless man, whose disloyalty had almost unhinged Tiberius, and drove him to such vicious acts. But Tacitus does record that not all Sejanus' friends deserted him, and quotes one man who had the courage to speak up for what he thought was right.

At a time when everyone else had hypocritically denied any friendship with Sejanus, a Roman knight, Marcus Terentius, who was accused of being his friend, was brave enough to claim his friendship, and declared in the senate: 'It would probably be better for me, in my present plight, to admit the charge than to deny it. Whatever happens, I will confess not merely that I was Sejanus' friend, but that I tried to win his friendship, and was delighted when I won it. I had seen him commanding the Guard with his father and, later, combining civil and military duties in the city. His own relatives, and his wife's, were given official posts. A friend of Sejanus was very likely to become a friend of the emperor, while his enemies were tormented with fear and humiliation. I mention no one person, but, entirely at my own risk, I will speak up for all of us who had no share in his final plans.

'We honoured him, not as Sejanus of Vulsinii, but as a member of the imperial families, to which he was allied by marriage, and as your future son-in-law, your fellow consul, your representative in state affairs. It is not for us to criticise the man you raise above all others, or your reasons for doing so. The gods have given you the right of supreme command; we are left with the honour of obeying. We only see what is in front of us, the men to whom you give wealth, position, the power to help or harm; and no one would deny that Sejanus was such a man. To enquire into the private thoughts or secret plans of an emperor is forbidden, dangerous – and unprofitable. Disregard Sejanus' last days, gentlemen; think of the previous sixteen years. We thought it marvellous if his ex-slaves or doormen recognised us! . . . Punish plots against the state or designs on the emperor's life; but since we gave up our friendship and respect for him on the same day that you did, that ought to acquit us!'

This brave speech, which reflected what everyone was thinking, was so effective that Terentius' accusers, when their previous crimes were taken into account, were banished or executed.

> Terentius' sentiments are very different from what one might
> expect from a free man in a free country, and illustrate how far life
> in Rome had moved along the road to tyranny. Some of the
> reasons why may become clear in the next chapter.

4 Treason

Treason was one of the earliest crimes to be the subject of Roman law. The law was rewritten on several occasions, but the definition of treason was never precise, though it was clearly some form of crime against the state. Under the emperors, the offence of treason came to include conspiracy against their lives, and even slander or libel against them. As Rome had no Public Prosecutor, information was brought to the legal authorities, or to the senate or emperor, by private individuals. If the evidence secured a conviction, the condemned were sentenced to death or exile, while the informants received one quarter of the estate of the accused, the remaining three-quarters going to the treasury. It is easy, therefore, to see how a dangerous class of professional informers developed, ready to bribe, to lie, to manufacture evidence, in the pursuit of riches won quickly and easily from the estates of wealthy victims. In the last years of the emperor Domitian, when Tacitus was sitting in the senate, the property of the condemned was seized by the emperor, and it is probable that many rich men were prosecuted simply because the emperor was short of money. It is hardly surprising that Tacitus' account of the treason trials in the times of Tiberius is distorted by his own feelings.

Treason trials first became frequent under Tiberius, and towards the end of his reign they spread terror among the senators and knights of Rome. But it is difficult to present a simple account of them. The first ones, in which Tacitus is trying to illustrate Tiberius's cruelty, in fact show the emperor dismissing foolish or trivial cases, or acquitting when there is doubt. Later, when Tiberius did mercilessly persecute many of the nobility, Tacitus merely gives a long list of the names and crimes, which it would be tedious to record here. So we have to try to recapture the menace felt by Tiberius' subjects from a number of unconnected trials. The first comments come from AD 15.

Early trials

Though the people repeatedly offered Tiberius the title 'Father of his Country', he rejected it, nor would he accept the senate's proposal that state officials should swear obedience to his decrees. No man, he said, could be sure that he was right: and the more power he had acquired himself, the more likely he was to make a mistake. Despite these remarks, Tiberius seemed as autocratic as ever, for he revived the treason law. The same name had been used in the past, but for different offences: if anyone in an official capacity deliberately harmed the state by, for example, betraying an army or plotting against the people. Deeds had been brought to trial, but words had gone unpunished. Augustus was the first to use this law against eminent men and women... Later when the praetor P. Macer asked Tiberius whether prosecutions under the treason law were to continue, he had replied, 'The laws must be enforced.' Tiberius too had been infuriated by the publication of anonymous verses attacking his cruelty, his arrogance and his disagreements with his mother Livia.

It is worth recalling some accusations tried out against two undistinguished Roman knights, Falanius and Rubrius, to show how this dangerous practice started and was skilfully encouraged by Tiberius; how it was checked at first, but then finally flared up and devoured everything. The charge against Falanius was that he had allowed a vulgar comic actor named Cassius to assist in the private worship of Augustus ... and secondly that he had included a statue of Augustus in a sale of some garden property. Rubrius was accused of swearing a false oath by the divinity of Augustus. When Tiberius heard of these cases he wrote to the consuls saying that Augustus had not been declared a god in order that this honour should be used to ruin Roman citizens. Cassius had, with other actors, taken part in festivals organised by Livia in Augustus' memory. There was nothing irreligious in including Augustus' statue, or those of other gods, in the sale of any house or garden. It made no difference whether an oath was falsely sworn in the name of Augustus or Jupiter – the gods should deal with the wrongs done to them.

Not long afterwards, Granius Marcellus, the governor of Bithynia,[17] was accused of treason by his own financial assistant, Caepio Crispinus, and by Romanius Hispo. Hispo was the first of a professional class which was later made numerous by the miseries of the times and men's shamelessness. He was poor, unknown and impatient: by secret reports he crept into the confidence of a pitiless emperor, and later became a danger even to eminent men. By gaining influence over one man, he earned the hatred of everyone else. Other poor men followed his example and became rich: despised and then feared, they ruined others, and finally themselves.

Hispo alleged that Marcellus had told disrespectful stories

40

about Tiberius – a charge impossible to deny. The accuser chose to describe all the foulest of the emperor's characteristics, as if they had been uttered by Marcellus. Because the descriptions were true, it was assumed that the accusations were as well. Hispo added that Marcellus had placed a statue of himself above one of Tiberius, and had cut off the head of a statue of Augustus and replaced it with Tiberius'. Tiberius was so angry that he broke his usual silence to declare that he too would vote about the case, openly and on oath. This was to force the other senators to do the same. Some semblance of liberty still survived, even though it was disappearing, so Cn. Piso asked, 'When will you give your vote, Caesar? If you vote first I can follow your example, but if you vote last I'm afraid that I may mistakenly vote against you.' The question struck home: Tiberius' anger was replaced by toleration, and he calmly allowed the defendant to be acquitted on the charge of treason.

Piso's question was a brave one: by asking it, he demonstrated the absolute power of the emperor which Tiberius normally preferred to keep concealed.

Hispo's accusations are typical of many of those made by the professional informers, in that they were easy to make and hard to disprove. Such informers frequently became so rich that they were often informed against themselves when a quarter of their property became a valuable prize.

In AD 16, a rather foolish young man called M. Libo was accused of planning a revolution. Investigation showed that Libo had been encouraged to make indiscreet remarks by an informer, after placing too much confidence in some astrological predictions. Despite the triviality of the evidence, Libo was so frightened, especially when Tiberius put Guards round his house and rejected an appeal for mercy before the end of the trial, that he committed suicide. Tiberius swore on oath that he would have pleaded for Libo's life, no matter how great his guilt, had he not forestalled the verdict of the court, and he may well have been telling the truth. Tacitus reports another trial, in AD 17.

Treason by insult

Meanwhile the treason law was maturing. Appuleia Verilla, the grand-daughter of Augustus' sister, was accused of treason for insulting and ridiculing the deified Augustus, Tiberius and

Livia, and for being guilty of adultery, despite her connection with the imperial family. It was ruled that the adultery should be dealt with under the Julian adultery law passed by Augustus. Tiberius then said that insulting Augustus was different from insulting himself; any irreverent remarks about Augustus should be punished, while insinuations against himself should not be investigated. When a consul asked him what his view was of the alleged slanders against his mother, Tiberius was silent. When the senate met on the following day, Tiberius asked, on behalf of his mother, that nothing said against her should in any way be thought worthy of prosecution, and dismissed the treason charge. As regards the adultery, he begged that the severer penalty should not be imposed, and recommended that Verilla's relatives should follow traditional practice and remove her at least two hundred miles away from Rome.

> Tacitus records at great length the crimes and trial in AD 20 of Calpurnius Piso. He had been one of Tiberius' agents and a personal enemy of Germanicus. He may have been responsible for the death of Germanicus in AD 19 (see p. 30): he was certainly guilty of treason, for trying to assume command of a province and an army against the emperor's orders. Piso committed suicide, an end that many other men chose when charged with treason. They did so because if they were convicted, their property was confiscated and their family and descendants were left penniless. But if they anticipated the verdict by suicide, their families were allowed to retain their property, apart from the quarter that was given to the successful informant. The pressure on the accused, when justice was so uncertain, must have been intolerable. Tacitus says nothing more about treason till he reports the following case from AD 21.

Treason by poetry and prose

At the end of the year an informant brought a Roman knight, Clutorius Priscus, to court. He had written a popular poem lamenting the death of Germanicus, and received a gift of money from Tiberius. He was now accused of writing another poem while Tiberius' son Drusus was ill, to be published for an even greater reward if Drusus died. Clutorius had boasted about this in the house of P. Petronius, in front of Petronius' mother-in-law Vitellia and a number of other important ladies. When the informer appeared, Vitellia alone asserted that she had heard nothing; the others were terrified into giving evidence. As the damning evidence was more readily believed, the consul designate, Haterius Agrippa, asked for the death penalty. M'. Lepidus spoke against it. 'Senators,' he began, 'if we consider just this one point – the disgraceful words with which Clutorius has shamed himself and outraged us – neither prison, nor strangling, nor the tortures which are reserved for slaves are good enough for him. His crimes are scandalous; yet the generosity of the emperor, and senatorial precedents both ancient and modern, recommend mercy. Stupidity is not a crime, words are different from misdeeds. It is reasonable therefore to suggest a penalty which will adequately punish the criminal, and allow us to steer a middle course between softness and severity. I have often heard our leader complain that suicides prevent him from offering leniency. Clutorius is not yet dead: if he stays alive he will not threaten the state, yet we have nothing to learn from his death. His foolish efforts are unimportant and will soon be forgotten. There is nothing to fear from a man who confesses his sins to impress silly women rather than men. Let's banish him from Rome and confiscate his property – the same penalty that treason would deserve.'

One ex-consul agreed, the rest supported Haterius. Clutorius was taken to prison and immediately executed. This caused Tiberius to make one of his ambiguous criticisms of the senate: he praised their loyalty in so enthusiastically avenging a minor offence against him, but regretted that they had been so quick to punish mere words. He praised Lepidus but did not rebuke Haterius. So it was decided that in future senatorial decrees should not become law for nine days, and that executions should be delayed for the same period. But the senate was never free to change a verdict, and Tiberius was never softened by the delay.

> In another case, in AD 25, when Cremutius Cordus was prosecuted for publishing a history in which he praised Brutus, the assassin of Julius Caesar, and for describing Cassius as 'the last of the Romans', he vigorously defended his right to speak about famous men who had been dead for seventy years:

'We know them from their statues, which even their conqueror did not destroy: history cannot forget them. Everyone gets from posterity the honour he deserves. If I am condemned people will remember not only Cassius and Brutus, but me as well.' Then he left the senate and starved himself to death. The senate ordered the aediles[2] to burn his books, but they survived, hidden away, and were later republished. How foolish it is to believe that the memory of future generations can be obliterated by the exercise of power today. On the contrary, genius gains strength from being suppressed: barbarous dictators, or their brutal imitators, only bring disgrace upon themselves, and fame to their victims.

Treason by friendship

From AD 26, with Tiberius permanently at Capri and absent from Rome, Sejanus' power had steadily increased, as we have seen. His hatred for Agrippina and her family was well known, and ambitious men saw an easy way to turn this to their advantage, as an incident from AD 28 graphically illustrates.

The year began badly when an eminent Roman knight, Titius Sabinus, was dragged off to prison because he had been Germanicus' friend. For Sabinus had continued to pay his respects to Agrippina and her children, making visits to her home and escorting her in public. Of all her supporters he alone was left: good men praised him for this loyalty, while her enemies hated him. Four ex-praetors plotted against him: they were all anxious for the consulship, but they had no hope of success without Sejanus' help, and only criminal action could win his support.

So they arranged that one of them, Latiaris, who had some slight acquaintance with Sabinus, should set a trap for him, with the rest present to hear what was said, and that after that they should launch their prosecution. So after a few casual remarks, Latiaris went on to praise Sabinus' loyalty in not, like all the others, abandoning a family in distress which he had supported in its glorious heyday. At the same time, he expressed his respect for Germanicus and his sympathy for Agrippina. Men naturally lose their toughness in misfortune, and Sabinus burst into tears; then he began to complain and, growing bolder, to heap abuse on Sejanus for his cruelty, arrogance and ambitions, and even attacked Tiberius. Latiaris let it appear that in sharing their dangerous confidences they were forging a close friendship. Sabinus now sought out Latiaris' company, visiting his home and confiding his sorrows to him like a trusted friend.

The four wondered how they were all to get to hear such remarks. Any meeting place must look private, for if they merely hid behind a door they might be seen or heard, or some chance suspicion might give them away. So three noble senators packed themselves into the space between roof and ceiling, a hiding place as sordid as their trick, their ears glued to any hole or crack. Meanwhile, Latiaris, finding Sabinus out in the town, hurried him home to his bedroom as if he had some fresh news to impart; after harping on the many difficulties of past and present he found new subjects for worry. So did Sabinus, but at even greater length – once sorrows come to the surface they cannot be suppressed.

The accusation was rushed to court; the four conspirators wrote to Tiberius to explain the history of the plot and their own degrading part in it. Rome was never more anxious or frightened: people said nothing, even to their relatives, avoiding any meeting or conversation with their friends; suspicious looks were even cast on dumb and lifeless objects like walls and ceilings.

> On New Year's Day, AD 29, a letter from Tiberius was read out charging Sabinus with plotting against his life. Sabinus was condemned at once and dragged off to the dungeons, his face muffled in his toga, bound hand and foot, the noose already round his neck. So much for imperial justice!

The reign of terror

> After the death of Sejanus in AD 31, Tiberius' suspicions had no bounds. He lashed out mercilessly. Sejanus' enemies too took full vengeance on his former friends. Men and women were accused of treason on the flimsiest grounds. Tacitus records executions and suicides one after the other, scarcely bothering with details.

These judicial murders drove Tiberius to a frenzy. He ordered everyone who had been arrested as an accomplice of Sejanus to be executed. There was indiscriminate slaughter. They lay there, men and women, young and old, noble and humble, in lonely solitude or piled in heaps. Friends and relatives were forbidden to stand by the bodies, to weep, or even to look at them for long. Guards stood around each one to note the sorrow of the mourners, never leaving the rotting corpses till they were dragged down to the Tiber. There they floated away, or were washed up on the banks, with no one to cremate or even touch them. The depth of terror had banished all human sympathy – compassion disappeared as brutality flourished.

> It is easy to accuse Tacitus of exaggeration, for perhaps no more than sixty-five people were harried to death in the twenty-three years of Tiberius' reign, and probably no more than twenty on

45

this one day. But imagine the storm of protest and horror that would sweep Britain if but one Member of Parliament were executed without a trial!

5 Provinces

While terror stalked the streets of Rome, and the Italians looked apprehensively at events in their capital, the rest of the empire, the provinces, mostly enjoyed untroubled peace and prosperity. By AD 14 the empire had nearly reached its greatest extent (see map, p. 4) – Britain was the only major addition to come. Perhaps the main problem for its rulers was to define and defend its frontiers. Tiberius was determined to follow Augustus' advice not to expand beyond its present boundary.

In Europe the Atlantic protected the coasts of Gaul and Spain, while the mighty Rhine and Danube rivers guarded the eastern frontier, with the Roman empire on one side, and the barbarians on the other. At the beginning of Tiberius' reign, Germanicus had campaigned in Germany for three years after the mutiny, without much success. Romans and Germans had learnt to respect each other, and stayed on their own side of the river Rhine.

In Africa the Sahara protected the fertile strip of land along the Mediterranean coast, though there were occasional raids by adventurous tribal chiefs.

In the east the Roman provinces in modern Turkey and Syria were close to the Parthian empire, which occupied what is now Iran. Here Rome experimented. There were some small kingdoms on the borders of her provinces: Rome overshadowed these completely, but she allowed their kings to retain their thrones in the hope that these 'client kingdoms' might act as a sort of inexpensive buffer between the provinces and the Parthians. (Parthia was too far away to be conquered easily, as Rome had found to her cost, and too difficult to hold even if it was conquered.) But the policy was not successful for long: the following example of the problems that arose helps to explain why.

Power politics in the Middle East

The year is AD 16: Parthia had been suffering a series of civil wars, and king after king had been killed in the struggle for power. The Parthians had grown into the habit of asking Rome to arbitrate by selecting their kings for them.

The Parthians started it. They asked Rome for a king, and accepted the one that was sent. Then, though he was a member of their royal family, the Arsacids, they began to despise him as a foreigner. This was Vonones: he had been given to Augustus as a hostage by his father, King Phraates. Phraates had driven Roman armies and generals out of his country, but showed Augustus every token of respect. To establish friendly relations he had sent him some of his children, not because he feared us, but rather because he distrusted the loyalty of his own people. After Phraates' death, his successors to the throne were killed off in a series of internal squabbles. Then envoys from the Parthian leaders came to Rome asking Augustus to let Phraates' eldest son, Vonones, accept the throne. Augustus was highly flattered, and sent Vonones off, loaded with riches. The Parthians accepted him with the pleasure that greets almost all new rulers. Later they felt ashamed of Parthia's decline in having to ask for a king from another world, who was tainted with the habits of their enemies. The throne of the Arsacids, they said, was being handed out like the command of a Roman province. The glory of the people who had slain Crassus,[18] and driven out Antony, was gone for ever if a man who for years had put up with being a slave in the household of a Roman emperor was now to rule the Parthians.

Vonones himself increased their scorn by rejecting the traditional pleasures of Parthian kings, hunting and horses: he was carried through their cities in a litter, and disdained their national festivities. They laughed at his Greek attendants, and at his habit of keeping even the cheapest household objects under lock and key. He was affable and easy to approach, but they were unused to these good qualities, and regarded them as strange vices. Because his ways were so unlike their own, they hated them, whether they were good or bad.

So they turned to another Arsacid, Artabanus, who had been brought up among the Dahae [east of the Caspian Sea]. His first attack was beaten off, but he rallied his forces and seized the kingdom. The defeated Vonones found refuge in Armenia, a country which was allied neither to Rome nor to Parthia, and which at this time was without a ruler... Its people were bewildered and disorganized. Since this was not so much a free country as one that was without its ruler, they put the exiled Vonones on their throne. But then Artabanus started to threaten them. The Armenians themselves were useless; to support

Vonones by force meant a war between Rome and Parthia, so the governor of Syria took him away. He kept him under guard, but allowed him to retain the title and dignity of king. I will recount later Vonones' attempt to escape from this ridiculous situation ...

Later [AD 18] Artabanus asked that Vonones should not be kept in Syria, because, with his agents so close at hand, he was enticing the tribal chieftains in Parthia to rebel. Vonones was moved to a town on the coast of Cilicia ...

In the following year Vonones bribed his guards and tried to get away, *via* Armenia, to a relative who was king of Scythia. He pretended that he was going hunting, then rode inland: a swift horse soon brought him to the river Pyramus. But the inhabitants had broken down the bridges on hearing of his escape, and he could not ford the river. He was arrested by Vibius Fronto, a cavalry commander, and then stabbed by an ex-soldier called Remmius, supposedly in a fit of anger. But Remmius had once been in command of Vonones' bodyguard, so it was suspected that he had helped Vonones escape, and had then killed him to avoid detection.

There are two more mentions of the unlucky Vonones. The first comes from AD 35.

Artabanus, king of Parthia, had been faithful to Rome and just to his people ... but later he became arrogant to us and cruel to his subjects, and despised Tiberius as an unwarlike old man. Anxious to seize Armenia, he put his own eldest son on its throne when its king died. He also sent us envoys with an insulting demand for the treasure which Vonones had left in Syria and Cilicia.

When the Shah of Iran fled from his country in 1979 the new government demanded the return of the riches he had stored in other parts of the world. The coincidence is striking.

The second mention of Vonones comes from the year AD 49, when another Parthian delegation visited Rome to ask the emperor Claudius that Vonones' *son* should be allowed to return to Parthia, to take over the throne from the existing king Gotarzes. Their reasons are illuminating:

'Formal terms of friendship have been accepted by both Rome and Parthia: we are your allies, and though we are your equals in power, out of respect we accept second place. Now you must help us. Our kings' sons are given to you as hostages so that, if we cannot tolerate the way we are ruled at home, we can apply to emperor and senate for a better king, trained in your ways.'

Vonones' son did go back to Parthia, but failed in his attempt to take over the throne. Instead he was taken prisoner by Gotarzes, who let him live, but cut his ears off. This was to demonstrate his own mercy, and to humiliate Rome.

Rome continued to interfere in the affairs of Armenia and Parthia; Parthia was equally busy trying to upset the peace of Rome's eastern provinces. It was not until the reign of Nero that a permanent peace was achieved.

Disaster relief

The next episode, from AD 17, illustrates Tiberius' genuine concern for the inhabitants of the provinces, and also shows that natural disasters were treated with a sympathetic efficiency that smaller and independent countries today find less easy to achieve.

Twelve famous cities in Asia Minor were devasted by an earthquake, during the night, which made the destruction harder to avoid and more serious. In such disasters it is usually possible to escape to open country, but in this case people were swallowed up when cracks opened in the earth. It is recorded that huge mountains were flattened, that what had been level ground seemed to rear up into the sky, and that fires broke out in the ruins. The city of Sardis attracted the most sympathy, for it suffered the worst damage. Tiberius promised one hundred million sesterces, and let the city off all taxes for five years. Magnesia came next, both in damage and compensation. The other towns were also exempted from taxation, and the senate sent an investigator to arrange relief.

Trouble in Germany

Trouble was always to be expected on the empire's Rhine frontier. Near the mouth of the river, Rome's influence extended eastward, to the Frisii, a German tribe who occupied what is now the Netherlands. They were subject to Rome, but never tamed. This uprising, which occurred in AD 28, is not in itself particularly important, but it is typical of the skirmishes that kept Rome's frontier armies always on the alert. It also demonstrates the convincing superiority of legions over auxiliaries.

In this year the Frisii, a tribe living across the Rhine, broke the peace, not because they objected to being ruled, but rather because of the greed of Roman officials. They were a poor people, so Drusus had imposed only a moderate tax liability – ox-hides for military use. No one had said anything specific about their size or quality, till Olennius, the district commissioner, who had formerly been a senior centurion, selected buffalo-hides as the standard by which they should be judged. This would have been hard enough for any nation, but was particularly so for the Germans, for though there are many large beasts in the forests, their domestic cattle are small. So the Frisii first lost their cattle, then their land, and finally their wives and children were forced into slavery. Their angry complaints brought no relief, so they turned to war. Soldiers collecting the taxes were strung from gallows. Olennius, anticipating their anger, took refuge in a fort called Flevum: considerable forces of Roman and auxiliary troops were stationed here to guard the North Sea coasts.

When the governor of Lower Germany, Lucius Apronius, heard the news, he summoned detachments from the legions, and specialist cavalry and infantry units of auxiliaries, and brought both forces down the Rhine against the Frisii. But the fort was no longer under siege, as the rebels had scattered to defend their possessions. So Apronius began to build causeways and bridges across the nearby marshland to get his heavy troops across. Then, finding a ford, he ordered some Germans who had taken service with us – some infantry, and one cavalry wing – to take the enemy in the rear. But the Frisii, in full battle formation, drove off the German cavalry, and the Roman legionary cavalry that had come to help. Then Apronius sent in three infantry cohorts, then two more, and finally all the rest of the auxiliary cavalry. These might have been strong enough if they had charged in together, but as they arrived at intervals they failed to reassure our shattered units, and were themselves swept away in the panic-stricken retreat.

The remaining auxiliaries were put under Labeo, the commander of the Fifth Legion. But when his men too got into difficulties, he sent to ask for the support of the full legions. However, the men of the Fifth charged ahead of the others, drove off the enemy in a fierce struggle, and saved the auxiliaries, who were now exhausted by their wounds. Apronius did not attempt to avenge his losses, or even bury the dead, despite the large number of officers and centurions who had been killed. Deserters later told us that nine hundred Roman soldiers fought on till the next day, but were cut to pieces in a wood. Another four hundred escaped to an estate which had belonged to a German who had served in the Roman army, but they killed each other as they were afraid of treachery.

The Frisii became famous throughout Germany. Tiberius concealed our losses: he did not want to fight a war, and give someone else the command of it.

> In truth Tiberius probably realised that the cost, in men and money, of punishing the Frisii would have been prohibitive, and that it was better to accept the losses, and keep quiet.

The phoenix

> Finally, under the year AD 34, Tacitus records a strange story from Egypt. Perhaps the strangest thing is that Tacitus himself found it credible, and thought it worth relating as something that other intelligent men of his day could believe in.

After the passage of many centuries the phoenix visited Egypt, an event which gave Greek and Egyptian scientists material for endless discussion about it. I will relate the facts on which they agree, as well as others which, though less certain, are by no means absurd. The bird is sacred to the sun. Those who have painted pictures of it are unanimous in showing that it is different from all other birds in its beak, and the markings of its plumage. But there is no agreement about how long it lives. A popular view is five hundred years. Others say it appears every 1,461 years, and that the last three that had been seen all flew to Heliopolis, the City of the Sun, in the reigns of Sesosis, Amasis and Ptolemy III respectively, accompanied by a flock of other birds, which were astonished by its strange appearance. The distant past is, of course, obscure, but there are less than two hundred and fifty years between Ptolemy and Tiberius, so several people have alleged that the Tiberian phoenix was not a real one, that it did not come from Arabia, or do any of the other things that tradition says it ought to. For when its years are over and its death is near, it is said to build a nest in its own country, and to spread over it some life-giving substance, from which arises a baby phoenix. The first task of the fully grown bird is to bury its father. There is a precise ritual. Having proved its strength by a long flight with a load of myrrh, it picks up its father's body, and carries it on its back to the altar of the sun (at Heliopolis), and burns it.

The details are obscure, and embellished by fable. But there is no question that the bird does now and then appear in Egypt.

The phoenix is probably merely the symbol of a cycle of time. 1,461 years is the length of the Egyptian 'Great Year', when the calendar year of 365 days and the astronomical year of $365\frac{1}{4}$ days exactly correspond, being 1,461 years of the former and 1,460 of the latter. Sesosis is otherwise known as Sesostris, who is confused with Rameses II who reigned in the fifteenth century BC: Amasis ruled c. 570–526 BC., and Ptolemy III died in 222 BC. But these dates are hardly helpful.

6 Care and concern

The twenty-three years of Tiberius' reign were as unhappy for the emperor as for his people. He was a gloomy and unsociable man, unable, it seems, to enter on any relationship of trust or friendship, even in his own family. Under him, the routine administration of Rome and the government of the provinces were fair and sensible, yet he was disliked and despised by the people, and the object of constant suspicion to the senate and, at the end, of hatred. But he deserves a better reputation. Though Tacitus makes no secret of his own abhorrence, he still lets us see, in the following incidents, the picture of a just and unselfish Tiberius, trying to do his best, clearly motivated by a sympathy for his subjects which it is not hard for us to recognise.

Justice in the courts

In the passage from which the first extract is taken, Tacitus has been describing, among the events for the year AD 15, Tiberius' interest in the proper conduct of the law courts.

In another case, a minor senator, Pius Aurelius, complained that the foundations of his house had been weakened by the construction of a public road and aqueduct,[19] and asked for the assistance of the senate. The treasury officials opposed his appeal. Tiberius came to his help, and awarded Aurelius compensation equal to the value of his house: the emperor was really eager to spend money on good causes – one good quality at least that he retained long after the others had gone.

Propertius Celer, an ex-praetor, asked leave to resign his senatorial rank on the grounds of poverty. Tiberius gave him a million sesterces – the minimum property qualification for a senator – on finding that Celer's own lack of money was due to his father's extravagance, not his own. When other senators tried to do the same he told them to prove their case to the senate: his liking for austerity made even his generous deeds look harsh. So the other senators preferred silence and poverty to the public confession that earned a grant.

Floods and games

In the same year the Tiber, swollen by continuous rain, flooded low-lying suburbs. When the waters subsided some buildings collapsed and lives were lost. So Asinius Gallus proposed that the Sibylline Books[20] should be consulted. Tiberius refused: he liked secrecy in divine as well as human matters. However the task of controlling the river was entrusted to Ateius Capito and Lucius Arruntius.

Gladiatorial games were presented in the names of Germanicus and Drusus. Drusus presided over them: he was much too fond of seeing blood spilt, no matter how worthless the blood was. The public found this alarming. Tiberius, it is said, disapproved, and stayed away. Various reasons were given – it was said that he did not like crowds; that he was naturally gloomy; that he did not want to be compared with Augustus, who used to attend cheerfully. It was also alleged that Tiberius

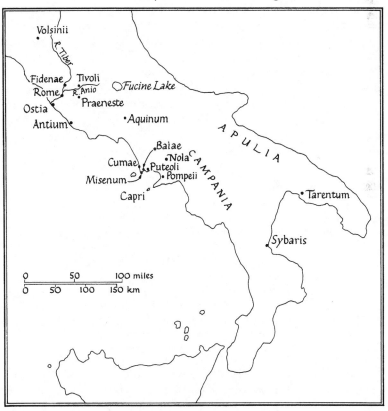

Roman Italy

wanted his son to be unpopular, and deliberately gave him this chance to show up his brutality, but I cannot believe this.

Riots

As long as the emperors ruled Rome, actors, and later charioteers, enjoyed the adoration now reserved for footballers and pop-stars. Violent behaviour at football matches is clearly no new phenomenon, and it seems that Roman officials were no more able to control disorders than the officials of today.

Hooliganism at the theatre, first seen in the previous year, became worse: some soldiers and a centurion were killed, and an officer of the Praetorian Guard was injured while trying to keep order and prevent the dignitaries from being jostled. The disturbances were discussed in the senate, and the opinion was expressed that the praetors should be empowered to have the actors flogged. The proposal was vetoed by the tribune Haterius Agrippa, and Asinius Gallus criticised him for doing so. Tiberius said nothing; he allowed the senate these shows of free speech. The veto was upheld – Augustus had once ruled that actors should be exempt from flogging, and Tiberius regarded his decisions as a sacred law. There were many regulations limiting actors' pay and the unruly behaviour of their fans. These are the most notable: senators were forbidden to enter an actor's house; Roman knights were not allowed to crowd round them in public; performances were to be given only in the theatre; praetors were given special powers to deport rioting spectators.

Religious scruples

The Roman empire embraced many countries, peoples, and consequently religions. All these religions were cheerfully tolerated unless they were immoral or in some way threatened the state. But the followers of these religions were ruthlessly punished if something wrong was done. In AD 19 a Roman knight assaulted a noble lady in the temple of the Egyptian goddess Isis, with the connivance of the priests. The priests were then crucified and the temple destroyed. At the same time a Jewish confidence-trickster persuaded another Roman lady to send gifts to the temple at Jerusalem, and then promptly embezzled them.

There was a debate in the senate about banishing Egyptian and Jewish religious practices, and it was decided that four thousand Jewish ex-slaves, who were of military age, should be deported to Sardinia, to help put down banditry in the island. If the climate killed them off the loss, so it was said, would be insignificant. All other Jews were to leave Italy, unless they renounced their unholy practices by a given date.

Tiberius reported that a Vestal Virgin must be selected to replace Occia, who for fifty-seven years had presided over the ceremonies with unblemished sanctity. He thanked Fonteius Agrippa and Domitius Pollio, whose keen rivalry in public service had led them to offer their daughters. The choice fell on Pollio's daughter, for no other reason than that her mother's marriage had lasted, while Agrippa had disgraced his family by a divorce: the emperor consoled his daughter with a gift of a million sesterces.

When the people complained about the terrible price of corn Tiberius fixed the price to the public, and gave the merchants a subsidy of two sesterces[13] a bushel. For this he was again offered the title 'Father of his Country', but rejected it, and harshly rebuked anyone who called his work divine and himself 'Lord'. Thus the orators had to steer a narrow and slippery path under an emperor who feared free speech, but loathed flattery.

Tiberius' administration

As we have seen in Chapter 3, Sejanus' influence greatly increased after he had regrouped the Praetorian Guard in a single barracks and started to win favour with Livilla. Tacitus chose to write a survey of Tiberius' whole administration at this point, believing that it was in this year [AD 23] that the emperor's character began to deteriorate. If we remember how much Tacitus hated the memory of Tiberius, it is clear that this grudging tribute is equivalent to high praise. After reporting where the various armies and fleets were stationed, he continues as follows:

I think it is a convenient time to review the other departments of state, and see how they had been administered up till this date, since it was in this year that Tiberius' principate began to change for the worse. In the first place, public business, and important private affairs, were handled by the senate; the leading men were allowed freedom of discussion, and if they stooped to flattery it was the emperor who rebuked them. When awarding promotions, he considered the nobility of a man's family, his distinctions in military service or any brilliant civil administration: it was acknowledged that he selected the best men. The consulship and praetorship retained their prestige: minor officials were allowed to exercise their authority without interference. The laws, apart from those concerning treason, were properly enforced.

The corn tribute,[21] indirect taxes and other state revenues were collected by companies of Roman knights. The emperor entrusted his own property to men who had been thoroughly investigated. Some of these were known to him only by reputation, but once they had been appointed they were rarely replaced, and most of them grew old in the same jobs. The price of corn was a great burden to the common people, but that was not the fault of Tiberius – in fact he spared no effort or expense to relieve the hardships caused by poor crops or stormy seas which prevented corn ships sailing. He made sure that no new burdens were laid on the provinces, and that existing ones were not aggravated by cruel or greedy officials. Flogging and confiscation of property were unknown. Tiberius' possessions in Italy were small, his slaves were kept under control, and his domestic staff was limited to a few freedmen. Any dispute with a private citizen was fairly settled in the law courts. Tiberius was never gracious, usually blunt and frightening, but he maintained this reasonable behaviour till the death of his son Drusus changed everything.

> But even after this, Tiberius' concern that the courts should be seen to act fairly had not diminished. In AD 24 there was another scandal for the gossip-mongers, which illustrates his continuing personal concern that justice should be done.

The praetor Plautius Silvanus, for some unknown reason, threw his wife Apronia out of a window. He was dragged up in front of the emperor by his father-in-law Lucius Apronius. Silvanus answered incoherently that he knew nothing about it because he had been asleep, and that his wife must have committed suicide. At once Tiberius proceeded to the house, and went to see the bedroom: there was evidence of a struggle, and that she had been pushed out. Tiberius reported the facts to the senate; when judges had been appointed, Silvanus was sent a dagger by his grandmother. Since she was a friend of Tiberius' mother, this was regarded as a clear hint from the emperor. Silvanus tried unsuccessfully to stab himself, then had his veins opened. Not long afterwards his first wife Numantina was charged with having caused his insanity with drugs and magic spells, but she was acquitted.

The emperor as god

> We saw on p. 56 how Tiberius rebuked anyone who tried to address him as if he were divine. One of the hardest things about

the Roman world for us to understand and accept is the 'deification' of the emperors. Deification means that the emperors were regarded and worshipped as gods. Julius Caesar and Augustus had, after their deaths, been declared divine, and temples were built to them. Augustus had even allowed a temple to be dedicated to 'Augustus and Rome' – the significant thing is that he had allowed this to be done while he was alive.

In the eastern half of the empire, people had long been accustomed to granting their rulers divine honours – a mighty conqueror, like Alexander the Great for example, seemed to them to have as much power as any minor god. These honours were granted as a token of respect, or gratitude, and did not involve the belief that the ruler really was a god. When Rome took over these eastern countries the inhabitants quite naturally wanted to award the emperors the same honours. Initially, this proved embarrassing, for hard-headed Romans had no doubt that their rulers were human and mortal. However, they gradually began to tolerate the suggestion that an honour which could be paid to a great ruler when he was dead might properly be applied to him when he was still alive.

At this time [AD 25] a delegation from Spain asked the senate's permission to follow the example of the province of Asia and build a temple to Tiberius and his mother. Tiberius generally despised such honours, and thought he should use the opportunity to answer the rumours that he was yielding to vanity. He delivered the following speech.

'I am aware, senators, that many of you regret that I did not refuse a recent similar request from the province of Asia. So I will explain why I did not object on that occasion, and what my policy will be in the future. The divine Augustus gave permission for Pergamum to build a temple to himself and the City of Rome: I regard all his words and deeds as law, so I followed his example in the case of Asia, all the more willingly because reverence for the senate was linked with worship of myself. One such occasion may be pardoned, but it would be sheer vanity to allow my statue to be worshipped among the gods in every province. Moreover, the honour done to Augustus will become meaningless if indiscriminate homage is paid to me.

'I am human, gentlemen, performing human tasks: it is enough for me to hold first place among men; I ask you to acknowledge that this is true: this is what I want future generations to remember. They will honour my memory more than adequately if they believe me worthy of my forefathers, careful of your interests, brave in the face of danger, and unafraid if my duties make me hated. These are my temples in your hearts, these are my most glorious and lasting statues. Monuments of stone are no better than neglected tombs if posterity's judgement turns to contempt.'

Disaster at Fidenae

In AD 27, the year after Tiberius had withdrawn to Capri, an emergency in the small town of Fidenae, five miles from Rome, reveals the senate at its best: they were perhaps glad to have the chance to show that they too were capable of acting as generously and promptly as the emperor.

In this year a sudden disaster, which lasted barely an instant, caused as many casualties as a major war. An ex-slave named Atilius started building an amphitheatre for a gladiatorial show. But the foundations were not laid on solid ground, and the wooden beams holding the superstructure together were not strong enough. Atilius had undertaken this project not because he had money to spare, or through any desire for personal popularity in his home town, but with the sordid motive of profit. Supporters of the sport had largely been denied such shows under Tiberius, and men and women of all ages flocked to Fidenae in greater numbers than usual as it was so near Rome. This made the disaster all the more serious. The building was packed, when it collapsed and fell both inward and outwards, throwing down or burying huge numbers of spectators and bystanders. Those who were killed instantly were at least spared any pain; they were better off than the injured, who remained conscious despite their mutilations, and had to watch their wives and children through the day and listen to their shrieks and groans at night. The news brought out the crowds, to weep for their brothers, loved ones, mothers or fathers. Any whose friends or relatives were away from home, even for a quite different reason, were sick with worry, and while the casualties were still unidentified uncertainty made their anxiety worse.

When the removal of the rubble began, people ran to kiss and embrace the dead, and there were frequent quarrels when similarity of physique led to confusion if the features were unrecognisable. Fifty thousand were crushed to death or maimed in the disaster. A senatorial decree prohibited, from this time onward, any person whose capital was less than forty thousand sesterces from putting on a gladiatorial show, and no amphitheatre could be built except on ground whose solidity had been verified. Atilius was banished.

The nobility opened their houses as soon as the calamity occurred, providing medical supplies and attention to anyone in need. And for these few days, despite the suffering, Rome was like the Rome of old, when after some great battle the wounded were supported with all the money or care they needed.

Fire

However, when major disasters occured, only the emperor could provide the money and organisation to provide long-term relief. Tiberius was quick to let the people see that his concern for their welfare had in no way been diminished by his departure to Capri. This account follows on immediately after the one above.

This calamity was still fresh in people's minds when an unusually destructive fire broke out in the city and reduced the Caelian Hill to ashes. People began to call it an unlucky year; the emperor's decision to leave Rome was a bad omen, they said, trying, as people will, to find someone to blame for what was merely bad luck. However, Tiberius answered this criticism by making grants to cover the losses. His action won him the thanks of the nobles in the senate and the applause of the people in the streets. For he made generous grants without favouritism to anyone who applied: it did not matter if they were unimportant, or made their claims by themselves without their family to plead their case.

Serious fires were quite common in Rome, with its tightly packed buildings still largely made of wood. In the last year of Tiberius' life another fire ravaged the Aventine Hill and destroyed the part of the Circus Maximus that adjoined it. He spent one hundred million sesterces on compensation for the houses and apartment blocks which were lost.

This was all the more popular because he had commissioned only two public buildings, a temple to Augustus and a new stage for Pompey's Theatre. And when they were completed he did not hold a dedication ceremony, either because he despised popularity or because he was too old. Five commissioners were appointed to assess individual losses caused by the fire: four of them were the husbands of his four grand-daughters, the fifth was nominated by the consuls. The emperor was voted every honour that ingenuity could devise, but it is not known whether he accepted or rejected them, for the end of his life was near . . .

The death of Tiberius

Tiberius considered who was to succeed him – there were three possibilities. His grandson, Tiberius Gemellus, was closest to him in relationship and affection, but was still only seventeen. Gaius, the third son of Germanicus and Agrippina, was in his prime, at twenty-five, and popular with the people; but Tiberius disliked him. Claudius, the brother of Germanicus, was thought to be feeble-minded. The likeliest contender was Gaius, especially as he had the support of Macro, the Prefect of the Praetorian Guard appointed to succeed Sejanus. But Tiberius refused to make up his mind.

Tiberius' strength started to fail him, though not his ability to conceal what he was thinking. His will-power and the directness of his glance and speech were unimpaired. Sometimes he tried to hide his weakness, obvious though it was, with an assumed cheerfulness. After moving from house to house he settled down in a villa on the promontory of Misenum.[22] He discovered that his death was near in the following way. There was a distinguished doctor named Charicles: he did not usually treat the emperor's ailments, but was there to be consulted if necessary. He pretended to be leaving on some business of his own, and clasped Tiberius' hand in a gesture of respect. Secretly he felt his pulse. But Tiberius realised what he was doing, ordered the banquet to be served again, and stayed up later than usual as though to honour his departing friend: he was probably upset, and so tried all the more to conceal his annoyance.

Charicles told Macro that the emperor was failing and would not last more than a couple of days. There was a flurry of meetings of officials in Rome: despatches were hurriedly posted to the army commanders and provincial governors. On 16 March Tiberius ceased breathing, and it was believed that his life was ended. Gaius Caesar came out to assume power, surrounded by a crowd congratulating him. Suddenly there was a report that Tiberius had recovered speech and sight, and was calling for food to regain strength after his fainting fit! Everyone scattered in alarm, assuming expressions of sorrow or innocence. Gaius was stunned, expecting the worst now that his high hopes had been dashed. Macro calmly ordered the old man to be suffocated under a pile of clothes, and told everyone else to get out. So died Tiberius in his seventy-eighth year.

7   Claudius

There is another gap in Tacitus' manuscript, after the death of
Tiberius in AD 37. The missing section covers the four-year reign
of Gaius (Caligula), and the first six years of his successor, his
uncle Claudius, the brother of Germanicus. Claudius, it is
thought, had suffered from polio as a child, and was left with some
slight paralysis. His physical handicap upset Augustus, who
would not have him in the court. Barred from public life, Claudius
devoted his time to studying the past, and acquired real respect for
Roman religion and tradition. When Gaius was murdered in
AD 41, Claudius was found hiding behind a curtain in the palace,
and the soldiers hurried him off to the Praetorian barracks, where
he was almost jokingly hailed as emperor. At this same time the
senate was discussing the chances of restoring the republic, and
they never forgave the man who had dashed their hopes. But
Claudius proved to be a surprisingly good emperor: polio may
have affected his body, but his sharp intellect was unimpaired. He
set up a Civil Service, whose various departments were controlled,
not by senators, but by his own freedmen:[23] this new organisation
contributed greatly to the efficient administration of the empire.
He constantly urged the senate to take its responsibilities more
seriously, and brought into it new members from the provinces.
Claudius' curiosity, his interest in past ages, and his regard for
tradition, are all reflected in this story from AD 47.

On discovering that even the Greek alphabet had not been
invented all at once, Claudius introduced new Latin letters, and
brought them into public use. The Egyptians were the first to
write down their ideas – they did so with animal-pictures. Their
records, the oldest in human history, are still to be seen, engraved
in stone. They also claim to have invented an alphabet. Then the
Phoenicians, who controlled the seas, brought the alphabet to
Greece, and took the credit for inventing what they had learnt
from others ... In Italy, the Etruscans[24] learnt writing from
Demaratus of Corinth, and the other early inhabitants from
Evander of Arcadia. The letters of the Latin alphabet are like
those of the early Greeks. They, like us, had only a few at first;
then more were added. Following this example Claudius added
three letters. They were used during his reign, but fell out of use

afterwards: they can still be seen in the bronze inscriptions that were put up in public places and temples.

Then Claudius asked the senate to discuss the formation of a College of Soothsayers.[24] 'The oldest of the Italian sciences', he said, 'should not be allowed to die out through neglect. Often when our country has been in trouble, soothsayers have advised us to revive old religious ceremonies, and to carry them out more carefully in the future. And leading Etruscans, on their own initiative, or encouraged by our senate, have kept up this science, passing it from father to son. Because of public indifference to proper learning, and the growth of foreign superstitions, it is being neglected.

'There is no danger at the moment, but we must show gratitude to the generosity of the gods by making sure that religious rites observed in bad times are not forgotten in good ones.'

A decree was passed that the priests should find out what institutions of the soothsayers should be preserved or reformed.

Wives and freedmen

As Claudius had been shunned by most senators before he became emperor, and had little experience of public life, he had turned for help and advice to his own freedmen, who had served him in the past, for they were shrewd and well-educated men, despite their humble status. They soon became important officials of state, the most powerful being Pallas, Narcissus and Callistus. Romans were quick to bribe them in the hope of obtaining their favour, for they retained great influence with the emperor. They acquired huge fortunes, yet Claudius' confidence in them was not misplaced, for they were loyal and efficient ministers. However, Claudius was not so lucky with his wives.

He had to divorce his first wife for immorality and suspected murder, and his second for more trivial offences. His third wife, Messalina, married Claudius when she was fourteen and he forty-eight. She bore him two children, but then lost interest in Claudius and took a number of lovers. This might have been overlooked, but when she went through a form of marriage with one of them, Narcissus informed the emperor and she was put to death. She was twenty-two.

The death of Messalina convulsed the imperial household. The freedmen started arguing about who should choose a wife for the emperor, for Claudius, who had been quite content to be ruled by his wives, could not stand the life of a bachelor. The competition among the ladies was just as fierce. Each one pointed out her own nobility, beauty and wealth to prove that she was worthy of so great a marriage. The chief rivals were Lollia Paulina, supported by Callistus, and Agrippina, daughter of Germanicus and Agrippina, who had the backing of Pallas. Narcissus favoured Aelia Paetina, who had been Claudius' second wife. Claudius himself was swayed by whoever had spoken to him last. He called the rival freedmen to a meeting, telling them to give their opinions, and reasons.

Narcissus suggested that the emperor would settle down easily with his former wife Paetina, the mother of his daughter Antonia, since he knew her so well already. Moreover, as she loved Messalina's children, Britannicus and Octavia, nearly as much as her own, she was unlikely to regard them with the hatred normally felt by a stepmother. Callistus argued that she was ruled out by the earlier divorce – to be chosen again would make her arrogant. Lollia was much more suitable: she had no children of her own, would be free from jealousy and would take the place of the children's mother.

Pallas said that Agrippina's greatest attraction was that the son she would bring with her was Germanicus' grandson, who was thoroughly worthy of imperial rank. He advised Claudius to link the Julian and Claudian families even more closely together, and not to allow the woman – who had proved she could have children and was young enough to have more – to give another family the distinction of being related to the Caesars.

This was the argument that won. Agrippina's own charms helped. She often went to see Claudius – a niece's visit to her uncle, she said – and he found her so enticing that she won the prize.

The invasion of Britain

Since Claudius had been kept out of public life he was always afraid that his lack of military experience and prestige might lose him the support of the soldiers. It was for this reason, as much as any other, that in AD 43 he ordered the invasion and occupation of Britain. Claudius won a triumph for the rapid conquest of south-east England – he came to Britain himself for sixteen days to preside over the capture of Camulodunum (Colchester), and renamed his baby son Britannicus. Tacitus' descriptions of the first campaigns have been lost, but we do have his account of another victory in AD 50. A successful attack had been made against the Welsh tribes commanded by Caratacus (Caradoc).

It was a famous victory. Caratacus' wife and daughter were captured, and his brothers surrendered. He himself found refuge with Cartimandua, queen of the Brigantes [who occupied Lancashire and Yorkshire]. But there is no safety for the defeated. Cartimandua put him in chains and handed him over to the victors, eight years after the start of the war. Caratacus' reputation was not confined to Britain; it spread through the provinces, and even the Italians talked about him. They were eager to see the man who had defied our power for so many years. His name meant something even in Rome, and Claudius, in exaggerating his own prowess, increased the fame of his captive.

The people were summoned as if to some great spectacle. The Praetorian Guard were paraded in front of their barracks in full armour. First in the procession came Caratacus' dependants, and his decorations and neck-chains, and the booty taken in war from his neighbours; next came his brothers, wife and daughter; last on show was Caratacus. In their fear the others turned to humiliating entreaties. But Caratacus held his head high, and on mounting the platform made no appeal for mercy, but spoke as follows:

'My family and rank are noble, and, if my prospects had been less impressive, I should have entered this city as a friend, not a prisoner, and you would have been happy to welcome me as a peaceful ally, a noble ruler of many nations. But as it is, my present situation is as degrading as yours is glorious. I used to own men and horses, arms and wealth. Are you surprised that I was reluctant to lose them? Must everyone else welcome slavery just because you want to rule the world? If I had surrendered without a fight, no one would have heard of my bad luck or your success. These will be forgotten if you punish me; if you spare my life, I shall be an everlasting proof of your humanity.'

At this Claudius pardoned him,[25] and his wife and brother. And when they were released they gave Agrippina, enthroned on another dais nearby, the same respectful thanks as they had Claudius. It was quite unprecedented for a woman to sit in front of Roman standards: she was ostentatiously flaunting her claim to the share in the power that her ancestors had won.

> Agrippina's influence over the aging emperor was growing continually stronger. Claudius had been persuaded by his freedman Pallas to adopt Nero, her son by a previous marriage, as his own son. Nero, now sixteen, was five years older than Claudius' own son, Britannicus, and naturally took a far more

important part in public affairs: he overshadowed Britannicus completely. There was no doubt in the minds of the people about which of them was more likely to succeed to the throne. Claudius seemed quite unaware of Agrippina's ambitions.

Public works and failures

The emperor's concern for his people was as strong as ever. In an attempt to produce more land for farming, in AD 52 Claudius drained the Fucine Lake, some fifty miles east of Rome. The attempt was only partly successful, and Tacitus appears to regard this spectacular feat of engineering more as an example of Claudius' vanity than as a serious project.

A tunnel between the Fucine Lake and Mount Liris was completed at this time. So that a larger crowd might come to see this remarkable achievement, a naval battle was staged on the lake. Augustus had done the same thing on a reservoir he had built near the Tiber, but on a smaller scale, with lighter ships. Claudius employed nineteen thousand men in triremes and quadriremes, surrounding them with rafts, to stop them escaping. There was still enough room for the crews to show their power and the pilots their skill, and for all the charges and fights of a real battle. Praetorian Guards and cavalry stood on rafts, behind ramparts, from which they fired arrows and stones from machines. There were marines in decked vessels on the rest of the lake. The banks, slopes and hilltops formed a natural amphitheatre, which was thronged with huge crowds who had come from Rome and the nearby towns to see the sights and to honour the emperor. Claudius, in a magnificent military cloak, presided: near him sat Agrippina, wearing cloth of gold. Though the battle was fought by criminals, they behaved like brave men. They inflicted many wounds, but were not forced to kill each other.

When the show was over the tunnel was opened, and the carelessness of the construction became apparent, for its mouth was not at the bottom of the lake, or even half way down. The excavation had to be deepened, which took weeks. To collect the crowds, this time an infantry battle was staged on floating pontoons, with gladiators. A banquet had even been laid near the outlet. To the horror of the guests, the force of the water as it broke out swept away everything near it: those further away were shocked and terrified by the crash and the roar of the water. Agrippina took advantage of the emperor's fright to accuse

Narcissus, who was in charge of the operation, of fraud and profiteering. He retorted by attacking her imperiousness and excessive ambition.

The death of Claudius

Two years later the antagonism between Agrippina and Narcissus reached a head. Narcissus accused her of adultery with Pallas, claiming that this was the proof that she was prepared to do anything to ensure the succession for her son instead of Britannicus. Indeed she was. But then Narcissus had a breakdown, and had to leave Rome.

Agrippina was quick to seize the opportunity. She had long ago decided to murder Claudius, and her agents were ready. But she needed advice about the type of poison. If she chose one that acted too quickly, her crime might be revealed: one with a slow or lingering effect might allow Claudius, if he realised her designs when his end was approaching, to turn again to his beloved Britannicus. She needed something subtle that would confuse his mind, yet would be slow to act. She consulted Locusta, an expert in such matters, who had lately been convicted of poisoning, but who now entered on a long career of imperial service. This inventive woman prepared such a poison: the eunuch Halotus, the emperor's food-taster, administered it.

All these facts were later so well known that contemporary writers revealed that the poison was sprinkled on some mushrooms, one of Claudius' favourite delicacies. But because Claudius was either sluggish or drunk, the effect of the drug was not immediately apparent, and a bowel movement at the time seems to have saved him. Agrippina was alarmed, and feared the worst. Risking the disgrace of detection, she resorted to the doctor Xenophanes, whose complicity she had already secured. He pretended to help Claudius by making him vomit, and, so it is believed, pushed a feather dipped in a quick poison down his throat. Xenophanes was aware that great crimes, though dangerous to undertake, are highly profitable when they succeed.

Meanwhile the senate was summoned; the consuls and priests offered prayers for the emperor's recovery. He was already dead, but his body was wrapped in blankets and poultices, while steps were taken to ensure that Nero would succeed him. In the first place, Agrippina, as if overcome by grief and in need of comfort, embraced Britannicus. He was, she cried, the very image of his father. She employed all her wiles to prevent him and his sisters, Antonia and Octavia, from leaving the room. Blocking every approach to the palace with guards, she issued frequent bulletins that the emperor's health was improving: she wanted the Guards to stay hopeful till the arrival of the favourable time predicted by the astrologers.

Then, at midday on 13 October, the gates of the palace were flung open. Accompanied by Burrus, the Praetorian Prefect, Nero came out to the cohort on regular guard duty. Prompted by Burrus, they greeted him with a cheer, and put him in a litter. It was said that some of them were doubtful, and looked about them, asking where Britannicus was. But as there was no one to lead any opposition, they accepted the choice that was offered. Nero was carried into the barracks and said a few words that were appropriate to the occasion. Copying Claudius' generous example, he promised them a gift of money, and was hailed as emperor. The senate's decrees followed the voices of the soldiers, and there was no hesitation in the provinces. Divine honours were voted to Claudius, and he was accorded a funeral in the same style as that of Augustus, since Agrippina was striving to equal the magnificence of her great-grandmother Livia. However, Claudius' will was not read out in public, in case the preference of the emperor's stepson to his son provoked a sense of injustice, of something wrong, in the minds of the people.

8 Nero and his mother

Nero was sixteen when, in AD 54, he succeeded Claudius. He
behaved modestly and sensibly, though perhaps the credit should
go to the restraining influence of Agrippina, and to the wisdom of
the advisers whom his mother had chosen for him. They were the
philosopher Seneca, and Burrus, the Praetorian Prefect. But soon
Nero realised that the real power was his, not theirs. When he
began to show signs of independence, Agrippina retaliated by
publicly professing her sympathy for Britannicus, and called her
son an intruder, who was using his position to maltreat his
mother. Nero was worried, but he learnt from her example. He
contacted Locusta, who was now in prison for her activities: soon
after, Britannicus was poisoned at a banquet in the palace.
Agrippina was alarmed and for a time retired from Rome.
Imperial policy was left in the hands of Seneca and Burrus.

Nero showed little interest in public affairs: he had fallen in love
with Poppaea, the wife of one of his drinking companions named
Otho, who was himself briefly to become emperor ten years later.
Poppaea's ambitions quickly grew: she wanted to be the empress,
not the emperor's mistress. However Nero already had a wife,
Claudius' daughter Octavia, and a beautiful mistress, an ex-slave
named Acte.

In the following year [AD 59] Nero at last committed a crime
that had long been in his mind. The longer he ruled the more
confident he grew, and he was falling even more deeply in love
with Poppaea. She did not believe that he would divorce Octavia
and marry her while his mother Agrippina was alive, so she kept
on nagging and deriding him. He was still mother's boy, she said,
an emperor who could only do what he was told, and could not
act for himself. 'Otherwise, why do you keep on postponing our
marriage? Aren't my looks or family good enough? Or do you
dislike my proven ability to have a baby, and the real depth of my
love? You're afraid that when we're married I won't keep quiet
about the way your mother bullies the senate, or how angry the
people are at her haughtiness and greed. If Agrippina can only
put up with a daughter-in-law who hates you, let me go back to
Otho. I'd join him anywhere in the world rather than share your

dangers and see your humiliation – I don't mind hearing about it.' Complaints like these, her tears, the way she played on his love, all had Nero at her mercy. There was no opposition, for everyone wanted to see the end of his mother's influence; but no one believed his hatred would go as far as murder.

The historian Cluvius records that Agrippina was so anxious not to lose her power that more than once, at mid-day, when Nero was already inflamed by wine and food, she actually put on a night-gown and offered herself to her drunken son. When the courtiers began to notice amorous kisses and suggestive caresses, his tutor Seneca sought a woman's help to fight a woman's wiles. The ex-slave Acte, already worried by her own danger and fearing for Nero's reputation, was sent to tell him that Agrippina was boasting about their affair, that rumours of incest were widespread, and that the army would not tolerate an emperor so immoral.

Fabius Rusticus, another historian, alleges that the initiative came from Nero, not Agrippina, though agreeing that it was Acte's shrewdness that broke off the affair. However, other historians and the traditional view-point blame Agrippina: perhaps she really did contemplate such an awful crime, perhaps nothing seemed beyond this woman. When still a child, she had, in search of power, committed adultery with one of the men who had conspired against the emperor Caligula; for the same reason she had later gone to bed with the freedman Pallas, Claudius' minister of state, and had completed her training in immorality by marrying her uncle.

Nero took Acte's advice, and avoided being alone with his mother. When she left his palace for her town house or one of her country estates, he congratulated her on taking a holiday. In the end he decided that, wherever she was, she was far too dangerous, and resolved to kill her. He hesitated only about whether to use poison, a dagger or some other means. His first choice was poison: but if she died at the emperor's table it could hardly be thought an accident considering that his half-brother Britannicus had been removed in the same way. It seemed too difficult to bribe one of her servants – she was so wicked herself that she was alive to any such ploy. Moreover, she had strengthened her resistance by taking a course of antidotes in advance. It was impossible to conceal a murder by stabbing – and an assassin hired for such a terrible crime might shrink from completing it. It was the freedman Anicetus who came up with a scheme. He had been Nero's paedagogus[26] and now commanded the fleet at Misenum;[22] he and Agrippina hated each other. He suggested that a boat could be constructed with a part that might 'accidentally' collapse when at sea, and thus throw the unsuspecting woman into the water. More accidents, he said, happened at sea than anywhere else; if she died in a shipwreck no one would be so unfair as to believe that wind or wave had obeyed human orders. When she was dead the emperor could build her a temple, and altars and so on, as proof of his respect.

This cunning suggestion was accepted. It was a convenient time, too, for Nero used to stay at the holiday resort of Baiae[27] during the festival of Minerva. He lured his mother there, remarking that 'one must humour one's parents, and put up with their bad temper!' – he wanted to spread the belief that they had been reconciled, and Agrippina, with the natural readiness of women to believe good news, to accept the rumour as true.

When she sailed round from Antium[28] Nero met her on the shore, took her in his arms and led her personally to a nearby mansion called Bauli. Among other vessels moored offshore was one rather more luxurious than the rest, which was obviously intended as another compliment to his mother, for she had been accustomed to travel in an imperial warship manned by sailors from the fleet.

She was then invited to dinner, so that darkness might help to conceal the crime. It has since been established that there was an informer, and that Agrippina, having heard of the plot, but doubtful whether to believe it, travelled to Baiae by road in a litter. There, Nero's attentiveness relieved her anxiety; he welcomed her warmly, and gave her the place of honour at his side. The banquet was prolonged, and conversation never flagged. Nero chatted lightheartedly, or put on a solemn look as if imparting important information. Then he accompanied her as she departed, gazing into her eyes and hugging her closely: either he was perfecting his hypocrisy, or else the last sight of his mother going to her death affected even his brutal heart.

The night was bright with stars, the sea quite calm, as if the gods were determined to reveal the crime. There were two friends with Agrippina: Creperius Gallus stood near the tiller, and Acerronia leant over Agrippina's feet as she rested, talking happily of Nero's changed attitude and his mother's return to favour. The ship had not gone far when the signal was given and the roof of their cabin, weighted with a mass of lead, fell in.

72

Creperius was crushed and killed instantly. Agrippina and Acerronia were protected by the high sides of the couch, which happened to be strong enough to resist the weight. The ship did not break up. There was utter confusion, for most of the crew were ignorant of the plot, and so hindered the few who were in the know. These then had the idea of throwing their weight on one side to capsize the vessel; however they took too long to agree on this emergency plan, and the rest of the crew kept the ship level by grouping on the other side, which gave the women the chance to drop quietly into the water. But Acerronia, foolishly shouting that she was Agrippina, called for help as the emperor's mother; she was finished off by boat-hooks, oars and any other piece of gear that was handy. Agrippina, though she was wounded in the shoulder, swam away in silence, thus avoiding recognition, till she was picked up by some sailing boats which took her to the Lucrine Lake, from where she was carried back to Bauli.

There she reflected that this was the reason for which she had received the treacherous invitation and been treated with such respect. She recalled that there had been no wind, and no rocks to strike on, that the ship had been near the beach and had started to collapse from the top, which you might expect some structure on land to do, but not a ship. Remembering how Acerronia had died, and eyeing her own wound, she realised that the only way of escaping the plot was to pretend that she was unaware of it. So she sent her freedman Agerinus to tell her son that through divine providence and his good fortune she had survived a serious accident. She begged him, no matter how upset he might be by her misfortune, not to bother to visit her yet; for the moment she needed rest. Meanwhile, pretending to be unworried, she put ointment and bandages on her wound. She ordered Acerronia's will to be found, and her property to be put under lock and key – this at least she could do without pretence.

Nero was waiting for news that the crime was concluded when word came that his mother had escaped with a minor wound, but had come so near death that there could be no doubt that he was responsible. Half-dead with fear, he insisted that she would appear at any moment to punish him: 'She'll arm the slaves and arouse the army. Or she'll go to the senate and people, and accuse me of wrecking her ship, killing her friends and wounding her! What can I do? Perhaps Burrus and Seneca can suggest something?' He had them woken up at once – they were probably well aware of the plot.

The result was that for a long time neither said a word, afraid that Nero would not listen if they tried to persuade him to leave her alive. Possibly they thought that things had gone so far that Nero had to do away with her first if he were to avoid death himself. Seneca at last took the initiative: he looked at Burrus and asked whether the troops could be told to murder her. Burrus replied that the Praetorian Guard was absolutely loyal to the whole imperial family: they had not forgotten Germanicus, and would do nothing to harm his children. It was up to Anicetus to finish what he had promised.

Without a moment's hesitation Anicetus claimed the privilege of completing the crime. At this remark Nero swore that only on this day had his reign really begun, and that it had been left to a freedman to bestow so great a gift. 'Hurry off! And take with you men who are prepared to do anything you tell them.'

On hearing that Agerinus had brought a message from Agrippina, Nero himself staged an act as an excuse to incriminate her. He threw a sword at Agerinus' feet while he was still delivering the message, and ordered him to be arrested as if he were an assassin caught in the act. His purpose was this – he could pretend that his mother had schemed to kill him, but had committed suicide in shame when her guilt was revealed. Meanwhile, news of Agrippina's 'accident', for so it seemed, had leaked out, and everyone flocked to the shore when they heard about it. Some climbed on the embankment or on the boats moored alongside it, others even waded out till only their heads were above water. Some stood with outstretched arms. The whole shore was filled with the noise of their lamentation and prayers, and their shouts as they called out puzzled questions or ignorant answers.

A huge crowd gathered, carrying lights; when it became known that she was safe, they set about sending her their congratulations, till they were scattered by the sight of troops marching up, armed and menacing. Anicetus put a cordon round the house and broke down the door. Any slave that met him was arrested: a few were standing by her bedroom door when he reached it, though most had been frightened away by the intruders. The light in the room was dim; only one servant attended Agrippina, now increasingly anxious since no one had come from her son, not even Agerinus. She realised that good news would have looked different from this. As it was, there was isolation, then sudden uproar and signs of disaster. Then her maid slipped away: 'Are you leaving me too?' she cried, and looked round to find Anicetus with a naval commander and a marine captain.'If you have come to see how I am, tell Nero that I'm better. If you are here to kill me, I won't believe my son responsible – he wouldn't have his mother killed!' The assassins surrounded her couch; the first blow to the head came from the commander's stick: when the captain drew his sword to cut her down, she cried, 'Hit me here', and pointed to her womb.

To this extent the reports agree, but it is disputed whether Nero examined his mother's body and praised her beauty. She was cremated that night on a couch from the dining room, with scant ceremony. As the pyre was lit her freedman Mnester killed himself with a dagger, either from love of his mistress, or fearing execution. During Nero's reign no mound or memorial was put over her grave, though later her family built her a small tomb by the road to Misenum near Julius Caesar's house, overlooking the bay.

Agrippina had accepted many years before that she would die like this, but had made light of it. When she had consulted astrologers about Nero, they had told her that he would be emperor, and put her to death: 'No matter', she said, 'so long as he becomes emperor.' As for Nero, he only realised the enormity of his crime after it was done. For some periods during the rest of the night he lay motionless, uttering no word; often he leapt up in panic, vacantly waiting as if he expected to die at dawn. Confidence returned only when, at Burrus' suggestion, the officers and centurions came to grovel, shaking his hand to congratulate him on escaping the unforeseen danger of his mother's attempt on his life. Then his friends packed the temples of the gods; nearby towns in Campania took the hint, and manifested their joy with sacrifices and deputations.

Nero, on the contrary, feigned sadness, as if regretting that he himself was unharmed, and wept for his mother's death. But though mens' faces may assume false expressions, places cannot, and the grim sight of the sea and shore there depressed him – some people believed they heard the sound of trumpets in the surrounding hills, and wailing from his mother's grave. So he withdrew to Naples.

Next, Nero sent a letter to the Senate: the gist of it was that Agerinus, one of Agrippina's most trusted freedmen, had been caught red-handed with a sword, and that she had paid the penalty of a guilty conscience for plotting his murder. He added accusations that had been made earlier: that expecting to share his throne she had wanted the Praetorians to take the oath of allegiance to her, and then to inflict the same humiliation on senate and people; that thwarted in this she had turned against them all – opposing his gifts to the soldiers and citizens, and threatening the lives of famous men; that only with considerable difficulty had she been stopped from forcing her way into the senate house and responding to foreign embassies. With an indirect attack upon Claudius, Nero laid the blame for all the sins of his predecessor's reign upon Agrippina. Her death, he said, was due to Rome's good fortune – so was the shipwreck. However nobody was stupid enough to believe that this had been an accident, or that a woman, just shipwrecked, had dispatched a single man armed with a dagger to break through the cohorts and fleets protecting the emperor. As a result, criticism was directed not at Nero, whose appalling behaviour had gone beyond all reproach, but at Seneca, for making Nero's guilt obvious by writing such a feeble letter of defence.

Nero delayed his return to Rome, uncertain how he should enter the city, and wondering whether he still had the loyalty of the senate and the support of the people. All the worst of his courtiers – and no palace ever had more – assured him that Agrippina's name was hated, and his popularity increased by her death. They encouraged him to return without fear, and find out for himself how respected he was; they begged leave to go on ahead. And they found the situation even better than they had promised – the citizens waiting to meet him, senators in their finest robes, women and children arranged in sections according to age and sex, stands built along the route as though for a triumph. Thus like the conqueror of a servile people, Nero arrogantly approached the Capitol,[29] and made the thanksgiving sacrifice. Then he plunged into the wildest debauchery, which, if not suppressed, had at least been restrained by some respect for his mother.

9   Boudica

As we have seen in Chapter 7, Britain had been invaded in AD 43 on the instructions of Claudius. South-east England, the most productive area, was quickly reduced to peace, and organised as a province, with the Fosse Way, stretching from Lincoln to Exeter, as its frontier. It may well have been thought in Rome that the occupation of the rest of the country was unnecessary. But raids into the province by Welsh tribes had to be stopped. Roman troops marched into Wales, and met with success when Caratacus, leader of the British forces, was captured. Rome also tried in Britain the policy of leaving client kingdoms intact to protect the frontiers. We have already met the ruler of one of these, Queen Cartimandua, who surrendered Caratacus to the Romans. Another was King Prasutagus of the Iceni, who lived just inside the Roman province, in Norfolk. However this policy failed in Britain too, notably in AD 61.

A major disaster occurred in Britain. Aulus Didius had become governor, as I mentioned, but made no attempt to occupy any more of the country. After him, Veranius made some unimportant raids into south Wales, but died before he could carry the war any further. Veranius was famous for his austere behaviour during his lifetime, but the final clause of his will disclosed his ambitions, for after some gross flattery of Nero, he claimed that he would have conquered the whole province for him if he had lived another two years.

His successor, Suetonius Paulinus, kept the country under firm control. He was an excellent general, the equal in military skill of Corbulo, who had won great fame by reconquering Armenia, and Suetonius hoped to win a similar reputation by victories in Britain – at least these were the views of the 'experts' who are fond of making such comparisons. Accordingly, he prepared to attack the Isle of Anglesey; its own considerable population had been increased by a flood of refugees. He built flat-bottomed ships to take the infantry over the short but treacherous crossing. The cavalry made their way over by a ford or swam beside their horses in deeper water. A mass of armed men faced them along the shore; between their ranks ran women, dressed in black with

Roman Britain

dishevelled hair like Furies,[30] brandishing torches. All around were Druids,[31] raising their hands to the skies and shrieking awful curses. This unprecedented sight dismayed the troops – they stood there unmoving as if paralysed, and made no attempt to defend themselves. Then, with Suetonius shouting encouragement, and urging each other not to be afraid of a pack of women and fanatics, they advanced, hacked down the opposition and drove them back into their own altar fires.

Afterwards, a garrison was set over the defeated islanders, and the groves where they had performed their savage rites were cut down. The Druids' custom had been to drench their altars with the blood of their captives, and to find out the will of the gods by inspecting human entrails. Amid this activity news reached Suetonius of a sudden revolt in the province.

Prasutagus, king of the Iceni, famous for his long reign and great wealth, had in his will made the emperor co-heir with his two daughters, in the belief that by such humility his kingdom and family would be spared. Far from it: imperial soldiers plundered his kingdom, imperial agents treated his personal property like the spoils of war. As a start his wife Boudica was flogged and their daughters raped. All the leading families of the Iceni were robbed of their ancestral property, and the king's relatives were treated like slaves, as if the Romans had been made a present of the whole region. Inflamed by this outrage, and in fear of still worse, since their country had been reduced to the status of a Roman province, the Iceni sprang to arms; the rebellion was joined by the Trinovantes and other tribes whose spirit was still unbroken. They formed secret conspiracies and swore to regain their freedom.

Their particular hatred was reserved for the Roman ex-soldiers, who had recently been settled in the *colonia*[32] at Colchester and had seized their houses and land, calling them 'captives' and 'slaves'. The other soldiers encouraged the veterans' lawlessness; their own way of life was similar; and they hoped for the same indulgence for themselves in the future. Moreover, the temple of Claudius [in Colchester] was regarded by the Britons as evidence that they would never be free. Those who had been selected as its priests had to pour out their whole fortunes in the name of religion. And it seemed easy to them to destroy a colony without walls to protect it – Roman commanders had been concerned more with making the place attractive than with defending it.

> The next events recorded by Tacitus were obviously carefully stage-managed by the Trinovantes to alarm the colonists still further.

At the same time, for no visible reason, the Statue of Victory at Colchester fell down; its back was turned as if in flight. Roman womenfolk were thrown into a frenzy, and prophesied the end of the colony, declaring that the cries of barbarians had been heard in the colony's senate house, that the theatre had rung with screams, and that a vision of the colony in ruins had been seen at the mouth of the Thames. Then the sea turned blood-red, and shapes like corpses were left behind as the tide went out: reports like these brought hope to the Britons and fear to the veterans.

Suetonius was many miles away, so they appealed to Catus Decianus, the procurator,[33] for help. He sent barely two hundred ill-equipped men: the colony contained a small garrison. But no ditch or rampart was built, nor were the old people and women evacuated, for the Romans relied on the temple to protect them, and some of their British friends were secret supporters of the rebellion who misled them and confused their plans. So they were as careless as if they were in a world at peace, when they were being surrounded by a horde of natives.

At the very first attack everything was broken down or set on fire, except the temple, in which the soldiers had concentrated: but it only held out for two days before it was sacked.

Petilius Cerialis, commander of the Ninth Legion, raced south to the rescue, but the victorious Britons routed his legion, killing all the infantry. Cerialis and the cavalry escaped to the legionary fortress and were saved by its walls. Catus Decianus was appalled by the catastrophe and the hatred of the provincials, for it was his greed that had driven them to war. He fled across the Channel to Gaul.

But Suetonius pressed on, quite undaunted, through the middle of enemy country to London; this was an important business centre, though not yet ranked as a colony. At first he thought of making it his base for the war; but reflecting on the small numbers of his troops, and warned by the grim fate of Petilius' rash action, he decided to save the province as a whole by the sacrifice of one town. Unmoved by tears or appeals for help, he gave the signal to march away, though he did allow anyone who could keep pace to go along with his forces. Those who were detained by frailty of sex or age, or by love of their homes, were wiped out by the enemy.

The same disaster struck St Albans. Boudica's troops, who revelled in looting but had no enthusiasm for hard work, bypassed any fort or garrison, and headed for the rich but undefended communities. In the towns I have named, it is established that close on seventy thousand Roman citizens and allies were killed. No prisoners were taken to be sold into slavery or ransomed; the Britons immediately hanged them, crucified them, cut their throats or burnt them at the stake, as if determined to exact vengeance before having to pay the penalty themselves.

By now Suetonius had collected the Fourteenth Legion, detachments from the Twentieth and the nearest auxiliaries, a total of ten thousand armed men, and prepared to join battle without further delay. He chose a position where his path ran into a wooded valley, making sure that he could not be surrounded and that the enemy could attack only over the open plain. The legions, in close formation, held the centre, with auxiliaries on each side and the cavalry on the flanks. Groups of British infantry and cavalry, in greater numbers than ever before, wandered at random, so fiercely confident that they had brought their wives along to watch their victory, sitting them in wagons round the battlefield.

Boudica had her daughters in front of her on her chariot, and as she rode past each tribe she recalled that the British were used to being commanded by a woman; but now, she cried, she was not there as a queen of noble family, defending her throne and possessions, but as an ordinary woman seeking vengeance for her lost liberty, her lacerated body and violated daughters. 'Roman lust has reached the point where they defile our bodies, old or young and pure alike. The gods will give us the revenge we deserve. Their Ninth Legion, which dared to fight, has been destroyed: the rest are skulking in their fortresses or looking over their shoulders for ways to escape. We are so strong that they will cave in at our battle cry, let alone a charge, or close combat. Consider our huge forces. Consider the reasons we have for fighting: at the end of the coming battle we must be victorious, or dead. That is my decision, as a woman. You men can live in slavery, if you wish.'

At such a critical moment not even Suetonius kept silent: despite his confidence in the courage of his troops, he appealed to them to disregard the natives' shouts and empty threats. 'There are more women than warriors to be seen in their ranks. Unfit for war and ill-equipped, they will run at the very sight of the swords and courage of the soldiers that have beaten them so often. Even in a group of many legions, it is only a few men who really win the battles – what glory there will be for you, when your small numbers win the reputation of a whole army! Keep close together, and when you've thrown your javelins, keep up the killing! Knock them down with your shield-bosses, butcher them with your swords. Forget the plunder – it'll all be yours when you've won!'

His words roused such enthusiasm that even the old hands, with experience of a score of battles, were so ready to hurl their javelins that Suetonius gave them the signal in complete confidence. At first the legions stayed still, protected by the narrow valley: as the enemy ran forward they hurled their javelins with unerring aim, then burst forward themselves in wedge formation. The auxiliaries charged just as keenly, and the cavalry levelled their lances and shattered any opposition they met. The rest of the Britons turned and ran, but escape was difficult because their ring of wagons had blocked their path. Our troops did not spare even their women, and their pack-animals, riddled with spears, made the piles of dead even higher.

It was a great victory, as fine as any in the past: in fact, according to some accounts, nearly eighty thousand died, while our casualties were around four hundred dead and a slightly larger number wounded. Boudica took poison. Poenius Post-umus, the camp commandant in temporary command of the Second Legion, which had not joined Suetonius, heard of the success of the other two legions, and realising that he had deprived his own legion of a share in the glory, and had disobeyed his general's orders against all regulations, he ran himself through with his sword.

Suetonius now collected together all sections of the army, and kept them under canvas to finish the war. Nero increased the Roman forces in Britain with two thousand legionaries from Germany, to restore the Ninth Legion to full strength [Tacitus says earlier that *all* the infantry had been killed, but many must have been left in Lincoln to guard the legionary fortress, and this accounts for the discrepancy in numbers]; he also sent eight auxiliary cohorts and one thousand cavalry, which were stationed in new winter quarters. Any tribe which was hostile, or whose loyalty was doubtful, was devastated with fire and sword. But the Britons' worst hardship was famine; they had neglected

82

to sow any corn as they were employing every man, young and old, in the war, since they were convinced that they could take our supplies instead. Moreover, these savage tribesmen were even less ready to accept peace because Julius Classicianus, the new procurator, who disagreed with Suetonius' policies, allowed personal rivalry to obstruct the national interest. He had let it be known that the tribes should wait for a new governor who would be neither angry from having fought them, nor proud from having beaten them, and would treat them mercifully if they surrendered. At the same time, he reported to Nero that there could be no end to hostilities till Suetonius was replaced: he attributed Suetonius' failures to his evil character, and his successes to luck.

One of the imperial freedmen, Polyclitus, was sent to investigate: Nero hoped that his influence would not only reconcile governor and procurator, but also induce the rebellious natives to accept peace. Polyclitus burdened Italy and Germany with the cost of his enormous escort, and, when he crossed the Channel, was equally successful in striking terror even into our own soldiers. But the enemy thought he was a joke. They were still independent and had not yet learned of the power of these freedmen. They could not understand how the general and army that had won so great a war could owe obedience to an ex-slave.

The real state of affairs was toned down in Polyclitus' report. Suetonius was kept in office to end the war, but when he lost a few ships and their crews on the coast, he was told to hand over his command on the grounds that the war was *not* completed. His successor, Petronius Turpilianus, did nothing to provoke the enemy, who in turn did nothing to annoy him. He applied the honourable word 'peace' to what was idle inactivity.

10 The great fire

Immediately after the death of Agrippina in AD 59, Nero divorced Octavia and married Poppaea. Burrus died, and was replaced by Tigellinus, an evil man who encouraged Nero's debauchery. Seneca retired in AD 62. With all restraint removed, Nero gave himself up to his pleasures, which were by no means all worthless. He loved horses, and delighted in driving a four-horse chariot. He wrote poetry and songs, and gave public performances, accompanying himself on the lyre. He believed that he was a first-class athlete – for who would dare to beat him? – and opened a gymnasium where the oil with which the athletes rubbed themselves was given to them free of charge. But his pleasures cost money, which his subjects had to provide. His extravagance, and his open delight in his power, made him unpopular. So did the reduction in the weight of the gold coinage, and the confiscation of private property, measures which he introduced to help pay for the war in Britain. His immorality shocked the citizens, especially as he made no attempt to conceal it. Tigellinus gave a notorious banquet where every sort of degenerate behaviour was openly practised, and Nero's reputation sank even lower. But worse was to come. The date is AD 64.

A disastrous fire followed. According to some reports it was accidental, but others claimed that it had been contrived by Nero: no one knows for certain, but there is no doubt that it was the most serious and destructive fire that had ever occurred in Rome. It began in the north-east corner of the Circus Maximus; as it broke out in some shops selling highly inflammable goods, it spread immediately, and fanned by the wind it engulfed the whole length of the Circus. There were no large houses or temples with grounds surrounded by walls, nor any other barrier to hold it back. The blaze first swept through flat ground, then spread uphill, then down again, destroying everything in its path. It moved too swiftly for any counter-measure; the city was at its mercy – its streets were narrow and winding, with blocks of houses set out haphazardly, just as they had been built in olden times. Besides, terrified and crying women, feeble old people and helpless children, everyone, whether thinking of others or only of their own safety, dragging away the handicapped or waiting for them, some lingering, others hurrying along – they all caused chaos. Often, as they watched what was happening behind, the flames swept past or in front of them. If some nearby district offered safety, it too was swallowed by the flames: another which had seemed far from danger was found, when they got there, to be in the same plight. In the end the people had no idea where to run, so they filled the roads to the country and lay down in the fields. Because they had been unable to save their loved ones, some of them chose to die, even though escape was possible – so did others who had lost everything, including the tools with which they earned their daily bread.

No one dared to fight the flames, as threatening gangs forbade it. Other men were openly spreading the fire with burning torches, crying that they had orders to do so – either because that was the truth, or because they wanted to start looting without restraint.

Throughout this time Nero was at Antium, and did not return to the city till the fire threatened the building with which he had linked the Palatine and the Gardens of Maecenas. But the fire could not be stopped, and the Palatine, with his house and its gardens, was overwhelmed. For the relief of the homeless refugees he threw open the Campus Martius and the public buildings erected by Agrippa, and even his own gardens on the Vatican hill. He had temporary accommodation built for the destitute masses. Food was brought from Ostia and nearby towns, and the price of corn was greatly reduced. However, these actions failed to bring him the popularity they should have, for everyone had heard the story that while the city was ablaze he had gone onto his private stage and recited a poem about the destruction of Troy, comparing the present disaster with the old one.

The fire was finally put out on the sixth day at the foot of the Esquiline Hill – a vast number of buildings had been demolished as a fire-break to fight the unceasing fury of the flames with open ground and 'empty sky'. But the panic had hardly subsided before the fire broke out again with equal ferocity in the districts which had been less densely built over. Casualties were fewer, but larger numbers of temples and pleasure arcades were destroyed. This outbreak caused greater scandal, for it had started on the estate of Tigellinus: the gossip was that Nero wanted the glory of founding a new city to be called Neronia.

Rome is divided into fourteen districts: four were left undamaged, three were levelled completely to the ground, and in the other seven a few buildings remained, but half-burnt and ruined.

It would not be easy to enumerate all the houses, apartment-blocks and temples lost, but among those of great antiquity destroyed by the fire were the Temple of the Moon,[34] built by Servius Tullius, the Ara Maxima and the shrine dedicated to Hercules by Evander, the Temple of Jupiter Stator that Romulus had vowed to build, Numa's palace, and the shrine of Vesta that contained Rome's household gods. Also lost were precious objects won in countless victories, masterpieces of Greek art, and records of genius from the past in their original condition. Beautiful though the rebuilt city was, older citizens remembered these many irreplaceable objects.

Some people noted that the fire had started on 19 July, the very day on which the Gauls had captured the city and burnt it [in 390 BC]. Others were ingenious enough to work out that between the two fires there had been 418 years, 418 months and 418 days.

But Nero took advantage of his country's ruin to build a new palace. It was remarkable not so much for its gold and jewels – till then the conventional examples of luxurious extravagance – as for its meadows and lakes, and the woods, open spaces and distant views that copied the countryside. The architects and engineers, Severus and Celer, had the ingenuity and boldness to try to produce artifically what Nature had declared impossible, and frittered away the emperor's wealth in doing so.

Proper planning regulations were applied to the rebuilding of those parts of the city not covered by Nero's new palace – something that had not happened after the Gallic fire. The rows of housing blocks (*insulae*) were placed at measured intervals and the streets were broad; the height of buildings was limited; there were courtyards inside the insulae, and colonnades to protect their fronts. Nero undertook to pay not only for the construction of these colonnades, but also for clearing the sites of rubble before they were handed back to their owners. Grants were given, in accordance with a family's wealth or position, for completing houses or insulae by a fixed date. Rubble was to be dumped in the marshes at Ostia by ships returning down the Tiber after off-loading corn. Wood was not to be used for certain parts of the buildings, only solid Gabine or Alban[35] stone, because this material is fireproof. Illegal drawing of water from the aqueducts by private individuals was stamped out, and inspectors were appointed to ensure a more abundant and more freely available public water supply. Every householder was to keep fire-fighting equipment in open view, not locked away. Semi-detached or terraced houses were forbidden.

These measures won general approval because they were practical, and also because they made the new city more beautiful, though some people believed that the former lay-out had been healthier, on the ground that the narrow streets and higher buildings had offered some protection against the heat of the sun: now, they said, in the broad and open spaces devoid of shade, the heat was fiercer.

These were precautions devised by men: now attempts were made to win the approval of the gods as well. The Sibylline Books were consulted: as a result prayers were offered to Venus, Ceres and Proserpina. Married women asked for the favour of Juno, first on the Capitol, then at the shore nearest Rome – seawater was collected and sprinkled over the temple and statue of the goddess. Women with husbands alive performed religious rituals, some of them lasting all night. But no human action, no generosity of the emperor, nothing done to appease the gods, prevented the ugly suspicion that the fire had been started deliberately. To suppress the rumour Nero found scapegoats, and had them horribly punished: they were popularly known as Christians, and hated for their abominable practices. The origin of the name was a man called Christ, who had been crucified during the reign of the emperor Tiberius by Pontius Pilate, the governor of Judaea. Though it had been suppressed for a while, this dangerous superstition was spreading again, not only throughout Judaea where the evil had started, but even in Rome. Everything disgraceful and shameful, no matter where it originates, comes flowing into the capital and flourishes there.

As the first step, self-confessed Christians were arrested; next, on their evidence, others were condemned in great numbers. They were found guilty, not so much of criminal arson, but of hating the rest of the human race. Their execution was turned into a comic entertainment: they were dressed in animal skins and torn to pieces by dogs; or crucified; or set on fire to illuminate the darkness when evening fell. Nero provided his Vatican estate for the show, and put on games, dressing himself in charioteer's costume and mixing with the crowd, or standing on a chariot. As a result, though they were guilty and deserved the ultimate punishment, the Christians became objects of pity, as if they were being punished not for the public good, but to satisfy one man's cruelty.

> Many pagan contemporaries believed that the Christians committed crimes such as incest, infanticide, even cannibalism – perhaps from a misunderstanding of the Communion service where worshippers partake of the 'body and blood' of Christ. Equally, they believed Christians 'hated the human race' because they had to avoid normal social gatherings or public amusements, which they could not attend without taking part in some act of pagan worship.

11 Conspiracy

The extravagance of Nero's new palace, and the fate of the Christians, had dismayed the Romans. A series of bad omens at the end of the year – frequent lightning, a comet, and so on – unsettled them even more. Though they did not know it, their fears were justified.

No sooner had the new consuls assumed office than a conspiracy was started, and immediately gained strong support. Senators, knights, soldiers, even women, competed to join – they hated Nero, and approved of Gaius Piso. He was a member of the Calpurnian family, which linked him to many illustrious families. Among the ordinary people he had an impressive reputation for his good qualities – or what appeared good qualities. He defended his fellow citizens in court with skilful eloquence. He was generous to his friends, and affable and courteous to strangers. He also had the luck to be tall and handsome. In fact his character was superficial and self-indulgent: he enjoyed anything frivolous, ostentatious or dissolute. But such qualities were approved of by the majority, who find vice too attractive to wish for an emperor with strict or severe morals.

However, the conspiracy was not the result of Piso's ambitions. It would be difficult to say who started it, when so many were quick to join. The leading spirits, though, were Subrius Flavus and Sulpicius Asper, respectively an officer and centurion in the Praetorian Guard, as the courage of their deaths proved. Lucan and Plautius Lateranus[36] contributed their violent hatred. Lucan was a poet, and Nero, who vainly fancied himself as a rival, had belittled his poems and forbidden him to publish them – so his reasons were personal. Lateranus' motive was nothing but patriotic love of Rome.

Tacitus goes on to list two more senators, seven knights, and four other Praetorians who joined the conspiracy.

But the real strength of the conspiracy was that Faenius Rufus, one of the Praetorian Prefects, joined it. He was an upright and respected man, and so less attractive to Nero than the other Praetorian Prefect, Tigellinus, a cruel brute, who persecuted Faenius with the frightening accusation that he had been Agrippina's lover and wanted to avenge her death. The conspirators constantly questioned Faenius till they were satisfied that he really was on their side. Then they began to discuss more seriously where and when they were to murder Nero...

Epicharis

Torn between hope and fear, they kept on putting it off, till a woman named Epicharis began to urge them on, and to censure their hesitation – no one knows how she found out about the plot, for she had never shown any interest in serious matters before. At last she grew impatient, and while staying in Campania tried to undermine the officers of the fleet at Misenum, and implicate them in the conspiracy. The affair started like this. There was a captain, named Volusius Proculus, who had been involved in the murder of Agrippina, and felt that his subsequent promotion had been less than such a serious crime deserved. Either because she was an old acquaintance, or in the first flush of a new affair, he told her what he had done for Nero, and how poor the rewards had been. He added spitefully that he was only waiting for the chance to get his own back.

This looked hopeful – he might be able to bring others in; the fleet could be useful, and provide many opportunities, for Nero liked sailing off Puteoli and Misenum.

Epicharis went a stage further. She began with a list of all Nero's crimes, including his abolition of the senate's rights, and explained how he could be punished for destroying the state: if Proculus played his part by bringing in his bravest men he could expect a fitting reward. But she did not reveal the names of the conspirators. So the information was worthless when Proculus told Nero what she had said. Epicharis was arrested and confronted with Proculus, but as there were no witnesses it was easy for her to refute him. However, she was kept in prison, for Nero suspected that the story was true, even though it could not be proved.

The conspirators were now driven on by fear of betrayal, and decided that the murder should take place quickly, at Piso's villa in Baiae. It was an attractive place, which Nero liked. He often went there because he could bathe or banquet without his bodyguard or any fuss. But Piso refused, protesting that it would look bad if the blood of an emperor, no matter how terrible, stained the table at which he was a guest. It would be better in the city, at that detestable palace built with the money stolen from his citizens – or in a public place, since it had been undertaken for the public good.

Murder plans

In the end they decided to do the deed on the Feast of Ceres[37] at the Circus Games. Nero rarely left his palace or its gardens, but he did go to the entertainments at the Circus, and he would be easier to approach while enjoying the performance. This was the plan. Lateranus, as if appealing for help on some private matter, was to fall in front of the emperor and clasp his knees. Lateranus was tough and big, and could hurl him to the ground and hold him there. While Nero was pinned down, the soldiers among the conspirators, and anyone else who was brave enough, were to run up and kill him. Flavius Scaevinus claimed the right to strike the first blow: he had stolen a dagger from the Temple of Safety . . . which he carried as an instrument dedicated to a noble deed. Meanwhile Piso was to wait in the Temple of Ceres, from which the Prefect Faenius and the others were to take him to the Praetorian barracks . . .

Betrayal

The secret was remarkably well kept considering that people of different class, rank, age and sex, and both rich and poor, were involved. But they were betrayed in the end, by events in the house of Scaevinus. On the day before the attempt, he had a long conversation with Antonius Natalis. Scaevinus then went home, and made a will. Next he took out the dagger which I mentioned earlier. Complaining that it was blunt from age, he told his freedman Milichus to sharpen it on a stone to a keen point. Then he sat down to a dinner, rather more lavish than usual, and gave his favourite slaves their freedom, and presents of money to others. He was obviously depressed and preoccupied, though he made light conversation, pretending to be cheerful. Finally he told Milichus to prepare bandages, and pads to stop bleeding.

Milichus was either in the plot, and stayed loyal up to this point, or, as was commonly believed, was completely innocent and only then had his suspicions aroused. He had the mind of a slave, which dwelt on the rewards for treachery, and the prospect of limitless wealth and power. Right and wrong, the welfare of his master and the freedom which had been his gift, were all forgotten. Milichus' wife, just like a woman, provided him with an even more sordid motive, fear: she reminded him that many other freedmen and slaves had seen what he had seen. It was pointless for one man to keep silent, when one man could be the first to reveal the plot, and reap the reward.

So at daybreak Milichus made his way to the Servilian Gardens. He was not allowed in till, repeating that he had grave and dreadful news, he was taken by the doorkeepers to the freedman Epaphroditus, and by Epaphroditus to Nero. To him he revealed the imminent danger, the seriousness of the conspiracy, and everything else that he had heard or guessed. Producing the dagger which he himself had sharpened, he begged Nero to have the accused man arrested.

Scaevinus was picked up by soldiers. He denied his guilt. 'This weapon, on which the charge is based, is a family heirloom, kept in my bedroom. It was stolen, by that ex-slave. And I often change my will – there's nothing special about doing so today. I have given freedom and money to many slaves before now. Today I did so more generously than usual, because I suspect that my will may be declared null and void if my creditors claim my property, for I'm short of money at the moment. I have always liked lavish banquets, and a comfortable life – I don't care what critics think. I gave no orders for bandages: his whole story is a tissue of lies, and he added this bit because it didn't need witnesses.'

Scaevinus' air of confidence made his words sound true. Turning to the attack, he called Milichus utterly dishonest and unreliable, with such assurance in his voice and expression that the accusation looked likely to be thrown out. But Milichus' wife reminded her husband of Scaevinus' long private conversation with Natalis, and of Piso's close relationship with them both. So Natalis was fetched: they were interrogated separately about their conversation, and gave different versions. With grounds for suspicion they were put in chains.

Confession

At the sight and threat of torture they both broke down. Natalis knew more about the whole conspiracy, and had a more persuasive tongue; so he got in first, admitted that Piso was involved, and added the name of Seneca. Natalis may really have been an intermediary between them; on the other hand he may have been trying to win some favour from Nero, who hated Seneca, and was looking for an excuse to destroy him. Scaevinus was told of Natalis' confession, and either was equally faint-hearted, or believed that there was no point in silence once the facts had been disclosed, so he revealed the names of the other conspirators. Lucan and others denied the charge for some time, but being persuaded by a promise of impunity, and in the hope of excusing their long silence, they gave the names of close friends, and Lucan even named his mother.

Nero now remembered that Epicharis was still in prison because of Proculus' evidence: thinking that a woman could not stand up to physical pain, he ordered her to be tortured. But neither whip, nor fire, nor the bitter anger of the torturers at being defied by a woman, could break her. She denied every-thing. So the first day's questions achieved nothing. On the following day she was being dragged back for further tortures in a chair, for her legs, dislocated on the rack, could not support her. She took the belt from her waist, and tied it to the back of her chair like a noose. Putting it round her neck she threw her whole weight on it and throttled out the little life she had left. So a former slavewoman, despite her terrible ordeal, protected men with whom she was unconnected, whom she hardly knew, and set a splendid example, while free-born men, Roman knights and senators, untouched by torture, betrayed their dearest relatives. For Lucan and his friends gave away their former accomplices one after another.

Reprisals
Nero's panic grew steadily, though he had redoubled the guards around him. The whole city was put in gaol, so to speak, as troops manned the walls, and blockaded sea and river. Infantry and cavalry, including some Germans, whom the emperor trusted because they were foreigners, invaded public squares, private homes, local towns and countryside. Never-ending lines of chained prisoners were dragged along to the gates of the Gardens where they stood waiting. When they were taken in for questioning, a cheerful greeting or casual remark to one of the conspirators, or some joint visit to a party or a show, was taken as evidence of guilt. Interrogation by Nero or Tigellinus was harsh enough, but Faenius Rufus joined in savagely. He had

not yet been betrayed by any informant, so he behaved viciously towards his friends, to establish his innocence...

After the conspiracy had been betrayed, while Milichus was still talking and Scaevinus still hesitating, Piso was urged to go to the Praetorian barracks to test the attitude of the soldiers, or to the forum to sound out the people ... but he was not persuaded. He made a short public appearance, then stayed indoors, strengthening his resolution to meet his end. He died by opening the veins in his arm.

> So the sad story goes on. Lateranus was executed, by a Praetorian officer who was a fellow conspirator. He died in resolute silence, without saying a word about the equal guilt of his executioner.

Seneca and his wife

Next came the death of Seneca. Nero was delighted by it: he wanted the sword to succeed where poison had failed. The only evidence against him was Natalis' statement that he had been sent to complain of Seneca's refusal to see Piso when he was ill, and to say that friends ought to meet to keep up their friendship. Seneca, stated Natalis, had replied that conversation and frequent meetings were no good for either of them, but admitted that his own life depended on the safety of Piso. Caius Silvanus, a Praetorian officer, was told to repeat the conversation to Seneca, and to ask him if it had been accurately reported ... Seneca was dining with his wife, Paulina, and two friends when Silvanus delivered Nero's message. Seneca's reply was as follows: 'Natalis was sent to complain to me, on Piso's behalf, that I had rejected a visit from him. My excuse was ill-health, and a desire for peace and quiet. The only person whose health I regard as more important than my own is the emperor. Seneca has no gift for flattery. Nero knows that as well as anyone: he's had frankness from me far more often than servility.'

When the officer reported his words, in the presence of Poppaea and Tigellinus, Nero's chief advisers in cruelty, the emperor asked whether Seneca was preparing to commit suicide. Silvanus said his words and looks had been free from any sign of fear or sorrow; he was told to go back and announce the death sentence. The historian Fabius Rusticus relates that he returned by a different route, and called in on the Prefect Faenius. He told him of Nero's orders, and asked if he ought to obey them. Faenius advised him to do so. They were all stained with the same fatal cowardice, for Silvanus was also a conspirator, and was committing one of the very crimes he had conspired to avenge. However, he avoided announcing the verdict himself, or watching it, by sending in one of his centurions to tell Seneca he must commit suicide . . .

Seneca checked his friends' tears, and revived their spirits, by gentle conversation or stern rebuke, asking them where their philosophic calm had gone, where was the Stoic[38] resolve in the face of misfortune that they had acquired over the years? Everyone, he said, knew of Nero's cruelty. He had murdered his mother and brother: the death of his tutor and teacher was the only thing left to him. With these and similar words, clearly meant for publication, Seneca embraced his wife, and with a softness quite unlike his previous firmness, begged her not to grieve too much or too long. He suggested that she should find some comfort for the loss of her husband in remembering the honourable way in which he had spent his life. But she declared that she too meant to die, and demanded to be executed. Seneca did not oppose her noble decision: he had no wish to leave her alone to suffer misfortune, and said affectionately, 'I have shown you how you may make your life easy, but you have preferred death and glory. I will not grudge you such a fine example. I trust we can die with equal bravery, but yours is the finer death.'

> Both of them cut into their veins with a single stroke. Seneca was slow to die, and opened the veins in his ankles as well. Afraid that his pain might weaken his wife's determination, he asked her to go into another bedroom. Then he took poison to hurry his end, still without effect. Finally he suffocated in a vapour-bath.

Nero had no personal hatred for Paulina, and to avoid a reputation for cruelty he had ordered her suicide to be prevented. So the slaves and freedmen, on the soldiers' instructions, bandaged her arms and stopped the bleeding. She was probably unaware of what was happening . . . But people prefer uncharitable stories: there was a belief that she had welcomed the fame of sharing her husband's death as long as she thought that Nero was implacable; then, when she was given a softer option, she was overcome by the pleasures of life. She lived on for a few years, with commendable loyalty to her husband's memory. Her face and limbs were very pale, which proves how much blood she had lost.

> The investigations continued. Faenius Rufus was at last betrayed, by Scaevinus, actually in Nero's presence. The Praetorian officer

Subrius Flavus, one of the conspiracy's 'leading spirits', admitted his guilt with pride.

Asked by Nero why he had forgotten his military oath, he answered, 'I hated you! No soldier was more faithful than me while you deserved my affection. I began hating you after the murder of your mother and wife, when you became charioteer, actor and fire-raiser.' I have quoted his actual words, because they were not widely known like Seneca's; but the soldier's blunt and vivid remarks deserve equal publicity. Nothing in the whole conspiracy made a greater impression on Nero. He was ready to commit crimes, but quite unaccustomed to hearing them criticised.

Executions went on and on. Natalis and Proculus were pardoned, for giving information so quickly. Milichus was richly rewarded. Silvanus was acquitted, but committed suicide. Lucan cut his veins, and while his blood ebbed away quoted some verses he had written about a wounded soldier who met a similar death. The Praetorian Guard were rewarded with two thousand sesterces[13] a head. An ex-consul, Petronius Turpilianus, and Tigellinus were awarded honorary triumphs. Nero made a speech, thanking the senate. After it he issued copies of the informers' statements and the confessions of the convicted in case he were accused of unjustified executions. And three years later he killed himself, in fear of the fate in store for him when he heard that the armies were marching on Rome.

Nero's character was undoubtedly greatly affected and moulded by the unnatural tensions in which he grew up. He was born to an ambitious and domineering mother, in the same year in which her brother Gaius became emperor. Almost his first memory must have been the banishment of his mother, when she was suspected of plotting against the emperor. Nero's father died a year later, when he was still only three, so while his mother was in exile he was brought up, almost in poverty, by his aunt. Agrippina was recalled to the court by Claudius, whom she married in AD 49. At the age of twelve, Nero then became the centre of her ambitions, but not as a beloved son. For his mother hoped that, as soon as her senile husband died, she could secure the succession for her son: if she could not occupy the throne herself, she would at least be a very great power behind it.

But his absolute power corrupted Nero, and made him vain, arrogant and over-confident: he dispensed with his mother. Then jealous fears of rivals, whether they were in poetry, athletics or military reputation, drove him to persecution and murder. This ruthlessness, and his constant immature debauchery, lost him all the popular support he had enjoyed at the beginning of his reign. In Rome and Italy, at least, he died unlamented. But his achievements in the arts, in diplomacy and administration – for example the rebuilding of Rome – are not insignificant. In the year following his death there was civil war again. Four army commanders in succession marched their troops into Rome and seized the throne. This 'year of the four emperors' – AD 69 – is described by Tacitus in another book, entitled *The Histories*. The people must have longed to have Nero back, with all his faults.

In some ways Nero was like the empire itself. It was far from what people wanted, and even frightening, but it worked. And anything else was so much worse.

Notes

1 **senate** The senate was the council of senior citizens and ex-magistrates, which took over supreme power in Rome after the expulsion of the kings, in 509 BC. Traditionally it began with one hundred members, soon increased to three hundred. Julius Caesar raised its numbers to nine hundred, Augustus reduced it to six hundred. Its members were forbidden to take part in trade.

2 **junior magistrates** These were the *aediles* and *quaestors*. The four aediles looked after the city's streets, markets, public buildings, water supply and public games. The sixteen or so quaestors helped supervise Rome's finances, fleets and corn supply.

3 **consuls** The consuls were the senior magistrates. They supervised the senate, commanded armies and governed provinces.

4 **praetors** The praetors were important officials, ranking below consuls, but performing much the same duties; they were also the chief legal officers.

5 **principate** The principate is the rule of the *princeps*, simply another name for the emperor.

6 **legion** The legion was the largest unit of the army, containing between five and six thousand men. There were ten *cohorts* in a legion, and each cohort was divided into six *centuries*. Only Roman citizens could serve as legionaries; they were highly trained in a number of practical skills, e.g. surveying, as well as in fighting. There were about twenty-eight legions in Augustus' army till AD 9; thereafter there were twenty-five.

7 **Quinctilius Varus** An army of three legions, commanded by Varus, had been wiped out in Germany in AD 9.

8 **Nola** A town some ten miles from Pompeii, where Augustus took to his bed after falling ill while travelling in Italy.

9 **Praetorian Guard** In imperial times the Praetorian Guard was the personal bodyguard of the emperors. See p. 31.

10 **auxiliaries** These were non-Roman soldiers, less highly trained and paid than legionaries. They were granted citizenship at the end of their service. They were organised in cohorts of five hundred or one thousand men. There were, in total, roughly the same number of auxiliaries as of legionaries.

11 **centurion** The non-commissioned officer in command of a century. They were regarded as the backbone of the army.

12 **farm** On discharge from the army soldiers were often given farms instead of pensions. This was often unpopular, as the farms could be poor land, in remote countries.

13 **denarius** A silver coin. It was worth four *sesterces*, the usual coin in which even large sums were reckoned. Caesar's soldier's received 225 denarii a year, and this rate of annual pay was unchanged till Domitian raised it, c.AD 90, to 300 denarii. About a third of a soldier's pay was spent on his

food and clothes. It is very difficult to give modern equivalents: Cicero, c.60 BC, paid 3,500,000 sesterces for a smart house in Rome. As a very rough quick guide, it can be reckoned that there are ten sesterces to an English pound.

14 **standards** The standard of a legion was a silver eagle, mounted on a wooden pole, carried before the troops on ceremonial parades, and into battle. Smaller units had less impressive standards, but they were all treated with an almost religious respect by the soldiers. In a century, the standard-bearer was a non-commissioned officer, junior to the centurion.

15 **Vulsinii** Modern Orvieto, some sixty miles north of Rome.

16 **Gemonian Steps** They led from the Aventine Hill to the Tiber, and the bodies of executed criminals were dragged from them by hooks to be thrown into the river.

17 **Bithynia** A Roman province, in the north-west of modern Turkey.

18 **Crassus** and **Antony** Crassus was a member of a triumvirate formed by Julius Caesar, Pompey and Crassus in 60 BC: hoping to gain a military reputation equal to that of his allies, he led an expedition into Parthia, but was defeated and killed in 53 BC.
   Antony was Octavian's colleague, and later his rival. In 36 BC he led an expedition into Parthia which ended in a disastrous retreat.

19 **aqueduct** There were eleven aqueducts in Augustus' time, supplying Rome with sixty million litres of water a day. They were marvellous feats of engineering, bringing water into the city through tunnels, or by channels carried over valleys on superb arched bridges.

20 **Sibylline Books** These contained collections of prophecies which could be consulted in national emergencies. Tarquinius Priscus, the fifth king of Rome, is said to have purchased them. When they were destroyed by fire in 83 BC, a new collection was made from various sources.

21 **corn tribute** The provinces had to supply corn for Roman troops stationed within their borders. For frontiers provinces, with large armies, it could be a heavy burden.

22 **Misenum** A promontory near Naples, where a Roman fleet was based. There were several popular holiday resorts nearby, such as Baiae.

23 **freedmen** The name given to slaves who had been freed. They occupied all positions in society, from the lowest to nearly the highest. Claudius' freedmen, for example, acted almost as ministers of state.

24 **Etruscans** A people living north of Rome, in modern Tuscany, who had been Rome's rivals, in early times, for the leadership of Italy. They were said to have been skilled in the art of divining the future, an art which was officially practised in Rome by **haruspices,** soothsayers. They worked by inspecting the entrails of animals, by observing prodigies (unusual births or growths, e.g. an animal with two heads), or by counting the number of lightning flashes.

25 **pardoned him** There is an anecdote about Caratacus, recorded by Zonaras, a Byzantine priest in the fifth century AD. He tells that Caratacus, walking around Rome after his release, and admiring the wonders he saw, exclaimed, 'Why on earth, when you have all this, do you want our miserable tents?'

26 **paedagogus** The slave who carried a boy's books to and from school was called a paedagogus. The term was later used of the schoolmaster himself.

27 **Baiae** A holiday resort very close to Misenum. The Lucrine Lake was a lagoon adjoining it. Bauli was a villa at Baiae owned by Nero.

28 **Antium** Modern Anzio; it was a small coastal town, some twenty-five miles south of Ostia, the port of Rome.

29 **Capitol** The Capitol Hill in Rome was crowned by a great temple to Jupiter.

30 **Furies** Mythical creatures, of fearsome appearance, who were said to haunt and punish wrongdoers.

31 **Druids** The priests of the ancient Celts, in Britain, Gaul and Germany. Anglesey was a sacred centre of their religion.

32 **colonia** A town founded by the Romans in Italy or the provinces. Its citizens had full Roman citizenship; so in backward provinces, like Britain, they were towns of special importance.

33 **procurator** The financial agent of a province, responsible not to the governor, but directly to the emperor.

34 **Temple of the Moon** This and the other buildings named in this paragraph were all of great antiquity, dating from the earliest foundation of Rome.

35 **Alban stone** The stone from the quarries of Gabii and Alba, some ten miles from Rome, was harder than the soft tufa available locally.

36 **Lucan** A prolific poet. A long epic poem, in ten books, about the civil war between Julius Caesar and the party led by Pompey, still survives. It greatly favoured the republicans, and so did not find much popularity with Nero.

The Basilica of St John Lateran takes its name from the site of the mansion once owned by the family of Lateranus.

37 **Feast of Ceres** Festival games in honour of Ceres were held from 12 April to 19 April.

38 **Stoic** Seneca practised the Stoic philosophy, which instructed that undue emotion, or the appearance of undue emotion, should be suppressed, as distorting true judgement.

Index of extracts translated

All references, except the first, are to the *Annals* of Tacitus.

Index of personal names

Romans are generally listed under their most commonly used names, without any attempt to be consistent. Only Gaius (Caligula), of the emperors, is included: references to the others would be too frequent to be useful.

Printed in the United States
By Bookmasters